ENDORSEMENTS

Finding Profit

Finding Profit

✦

The Lean Manufacturing Journey to Profit for the Job Shop

John Macchia
Don Tapping
Cynthia Guy

iUniverse, Inc.
New York Lincoln Shanghai

Finding Profit
The Lean Manufacturing Journey to Profit for the Job Shop

iUniverse, Inc.

For information address:
iUniverse, Inc.
2021 Pine Lake Road, Suite 100
Lincoln, NE 68512
www.iuniverse.com

ISBN: 0-595-29616-5

Printed in the United States of America

Contents

OPENING LETTER

Dear Reader:

When I sold a part for $25.00 dollars that cost me $250.00 to make, I knew we were in big trouble.

Advanced Turning & Manufacturing, Inc., (ATMI) produces precision machined components for aerospace, aircraft, marine and pharmaceutical industries and is a small job shop. Like other successful job shops, we were proud of our ability to respond to customers' demands, proud of our quality and I'm embarrassed to admit, I was proud of our rework area. We were shooting at the right targets, quality and customer satisfaction, but using the wrong ammunition. While many other job shops are no longer in business, we underwent a change that kept us profitable.

We have always had the best employees; highly trained, competent and committed. We've always bought the latest equipment but our window of advantage was growing shorter and shorter as our competition also bought the latest equipment and our customer demands in terms of increased quality and price reductions continued. Our margins were decreasing. What we'd always done in the past to maintain our competitive edge wasn't working anymore. Our margins were slipping and showing no sign of turning upward.

On a personal note, my marriage was ending, my partner wanted out and I had a slipped disc that the surgeon said was going to require surgery. All in all, things weren't going well.

A customer called and wanted five more parts in addition to the order we'd already shipped them. The parts normally sold for $ 100.00 each. With a quick glance at our inventory list, I knew we had six parts in inventory which were an overrun of the customer's previous order. Since I always wanted to help out the customer, I agreed to sell the parts for $ 25.00 each. Having made an easy $ 125.00, I decided to take a little longer lunch after giving the order to our Operations Manager. This was found money.

When I returned an hour later than normal from lunch, I located the Operations Manager on the mezzanine who was *still* looking for the parts. (My longer lunch didn't seem like such a good idea now.) After digging around myself, I located the parts we'd kept in inventory and found five parts instead of six. One was tagged "hex oversize two thousandths, can be reworked" and another is tagged "thread undersize by one-tenth."

Three good parts, one part was completely worthless and maybe another one could be reworked. The customer was promised five good parts by tomorrow and for $25.00 a piece.

The Operations Manager assigned one employee to rework the part which required taking the employee off his present job, tearing down his machine and resetting for the customer's part while the Operations Manager was going to make a new part. That required stopping one job, idling an employee, resetting another machine for the customer's part, not to mention the Operations Manager's normal responsibilities were going to be neglected while he was working on my "found money" job.

I've personally committed to the customer rapid delivery on the part and selling the part for $25.00. When everything was tallied up, the new part cost me $250.00 to make, including materials, labor and time, and the customer was paying only $125.00 for the entire order.

If these kinds of problems existed with just one order, who knew what other problems were buried?

My life had gone into building the business and I was watching it crumble before my eyes.

This event caused me to take a long, hard look at what we were doing at ATMI and it was sobering. It was no wonder that our margins were slipping. Coupled with our own inefficiencies, the demands for increased quality from our customers as well as reductions in cost, the downward spiral was inevitable.

The problem was waste. Pure and simple.

- Waste of time
- Waste of resources
- Waste of movement
- Waste of space

I knew ATMI was profitable with the following equation: one minute = one dollar and we were so far out of range that back surgery seemed like a vacation. I went on a quest to remove waste and any non-value added activities at ATMI.

Let me explain the minute = dollar equation. When an operator was actively shaping the metal, we grossed one dollar a minute. So as long as our operators were busy doing the right things, we were making money: one minute = one dollar. However, during the long, hard, and painful look at my business, I realized that we were really only productive a fraction of the time. As I'd mentioned earlier, we purchased the fastest machines but what that actually did was allow more time for our employees to stand around. I am not faulting our employees. They did what they were asked. But, after a machinist starts a job, and has to wait for the machine to cycle before doing anything else, the waiting time is sheer cost. Our internal examination revealed that most of our jobs had a four minute cycle time. Machinists were busy for just one minute of the four. Taking the typical job and watching it go through an average of five operations, (four minutes per operation x five operations = twenty minutes), the operators were only busy five out of every twenty minutes. The rest of their time was spent waiting. Multiply those numbers by the number of operators, machines, processes and parts, and the loss due to waste was staggering.

It was the way we'd <u>always</u> done business. (It is also the way that most businesses operate.) But it wasn't working anymore. ATMI had to change to survive. I'll be the first to admit that if economic pressures hadn't forced the issue, we wouldn't have changed. The ability to adapt and change is something we're all very good at now at ATMI but the first bout of major change rocked us to our very foundations.

A major customer, Aeroquip had invited me to attend a seminar on Lean Manufacturing and with a great deal of reluctance, I attended. Before the seminar, I thought "Here we go again. A new set of buzz words. Plus, they're going to tell us how the big guys do it and it's not going to apply to the small job shop." I was dead wrong.

The principles of Lean Manufacturing were absolutely applicable to the small job shop, even though many of my colleagues and some of my employees thought I'd taken leave of my senses when I launched Lean at ATMI.

Every horror story, every Bogeyman, every "That only works for the big guys", every excuse as to why Lean wouldn't work for a small job shop were just that—excuses. One and all. It's amazing how hard the human mind will resist change and work to hold on to the old way of doing things. I've often thought how much better American manufacturing would be if people put in that same energy to making change work for them, rather than resisting it.

I won't tell you that our conversion to Lean Manufacturing was easy but I will tell you that it was necessary. I am firmly committed that Lean Manufacturing offers the solutions so many businesses desperately need. In part, that's the motivation for this book.

At the book store, you'll find dozens of books on Lean Manufacturing and some of them are good. But, they're all theory-based with only snapshots of real-life examples. Finding Profit is the complete story, start to finish, from old-fashioned manufacturing to Lean Manufacturing at ATMI. Lean Manufacturing works for small to medium manufacturers and job shops.

We're proud of our accomplishments at ATMI and are frequently benchmarked by other companies. A partial list includes:

- Classic Turning Inc
- Eaton-Aeroquip
- Mistequay Group
- Swiss America
- Ideal Forging
- McGill Manufacturing
- Eaton European Operations
- Stryker
- Williams International

I am deeply indebted to Aeroquip for inviting me to their Lean seminar. I've taken creative license with the people identified as attending the Aeroquip seminar. They are all fictional but represent composites of people who resist change.

Finding Profit is the story, told in parable form, of the transformation of ATMI through Lean manufacturing. It wasn't easy and if I hadn't been totally committed to the transformation, it would not have happened. I'd never thought to write a book but a consultant named Don Tapping convinced me that our story was one other small to medium-sized job shops needed to hear. There was a common myth that Lean was only for the "big guys" and would not work at a small job shop. We knew that wasn't true. While it's true that Lean was first introduced in the United States in the automotive industry, it is not true that it's strictly an innovation for automotive. ATMI is the living proof.

Please join us for the adventures of a company in trouble going through transition to solid profitability and growth; the story of a man, a boy and a beagle pup.

1

"Hey, mister, have you seen my dog?"

Startled, John turned around to see a young boy looking up at him. "Your dog?" John asked.

"Yes. He's disappeared." The young boy kicked a stone and said, "He does that sometimes and I want to find him."

"I know what you mean," John said. "I was looking for something, too. What's your dog's name?"

The boy told him the dog's name and said, "But I always call him Pro. He's a beagle."

"Profit?" John thought. The dog's name was Profit? Funny, he was looking for lost profit, too, as a shipment of bad parts that needed to be reworked was being unloaded on the dock.

"Boss, this shipment means we're working overtime and this weekend again," Ron Stabler, the day shift foreman said, as he walked up to John and the boy.

"Go ahead and do it. We don't have a choice," John said. "By the way, have you seen a beagle dog?"

"No, sure haven't," Ron answered.

"What's your name, kid?" John asked the boy.

"Jimmy. Sometimes he takes off. I think I know where he is but then he's not there at all," he said.

"I know what you mean," John said, thinking, *"Yeah, I thought there was profit in that shipment but no profit there."*

"There he is!" Jimmy yelled and dashed across the parking lot to the back field.

John watched as Jimmy ran to the beagle who was poking around the weeds at the edge of the field. When the boy was reunited with his dog, he turned back to Ron.

"What happened with these parts?" he asked Ron.

"I'm not really sure."

"How'd we ship an entire truckload of bad parts to a customer?" he insisted.

"Well, I had Hanson on the lathe and he hadn't run it before so it took him awhile to get up to speed. The specs said the parts should take three minutes but they really took seven. Also, the customer had changed the specs this time and the tolerances were tighter. We missed them by 5/100th. We were really rushed on the deadline so I had to double-team the guys to keep parts going. I thought we had some of the parts in inventory and we did, but not all of them were good and none of them matched the new specifications. Oh, and Carson couldn't find the diamond deburrer so he went through a dozen bits using the steel ones."

"So, you're telling me that we used the wrong equipment, an untrained and inexperienced lathe operator, twice as many people as the job called for and it took us twice as long, plus the inventory count is wrong?"

"That's about the size of it, Boss."

"Not quite. We have to rework what parts we can. Undoubtedly we'll be scrapping some and making more. And, the worst of it is we have a really ticked off customer."

"Well, we never made much money on that job anyway," Ron answered.

"At this rate, we'll paying the customer to take our parts," John said, as he turned into the building.

Walking across the shop floor, he saw thirty employees scurrying from one place to the other. What had once seemed a beehive of productivity now only seemed like chaos and confusion to John.

Heading down the hall to his office, he ran into Larry Myers, the sales manager.

"John, Aeroquip just told me they want a ten percent price decrease on their parts for next year. What do you want me to tell them?"

"Talk with Michaelson and find out if there's any way we can possibly meet their demands," John said as he continued down the hall.

As he passed Doug Maguire's office, Doug motioned for him to come inside.

"Look, John, I don't want this buy-out to take any longer than it has to. I gave you my counteroffer last week and I know what my stock is worth so just get out your checkbook."

"Did you know that we just had a shipment rejected from Aeroquip?" John asked.

"No, but that's not my problem. I just want to be paid what my stock is worth."

"You may not think this is your problem, but that kind of rejection affects the checkbook."

"Like I said,…"

Cutting him off, John said, "We'll have to talk about this later," and left Doug stewing.

He grabbed a cup of coffee before going to his own office. Eager for the solitude and privacy of his own office, he didn't make eye contact with anyone else as he headed for his sanctuary. But, Estelle Goody, his secretary, couldn't or wouldn't be ignored.

"John, your attorney called," she said. "Your wife's attorney has her divorce settlement offer and wants an answer today. He's faxing it over right now."

"Okay."

"He also said that her attorney is putting some pressure on and said the price will go up if they don't get an answer today."

"That's great. Just great," John said with frustration.

Opening the door to his office, he looked at Estelle. "Hold all of my calls and I don't want to be disturbed."

"But what if…"

"I don't want to be disturbed by anyone," he said as he went into his office. He softly closed the door.

2

The next morning, John was on his second cup of coffee when Estelle escorted Joel Eckstein, John's CPA, into his office.

Startled by Joel's appearance, John said, "Estelle, please get this man a cup of coffee immediately." When she'd left, John asked, "What in blazes is wrong with you. You look like death warmed over."

"Let me get my coffee first, John, before we get into this." Joel reached into his briefcase and withdrew a large file folder and placed it on John's desk. He sighed heavily and wouldn't meet John's eyes until Estelle returned with his coffee and exited the office.

"Joel, you look like you haven't slept in a week," John said.

"I feel that way, too. I'm beginning to feel like the Queen's executioner."

"Things are that bad?"

"Not with my firm. We're busier than ever. It's just that we're delivering so much bad news to clients these days."

"Including me?" John asked.

Joel nodded.

"Okay. Well, let's get on with it, then," John said.

Joel opened up the file folder.

"The last quarter doesn't look that bad," he began. "But when you consider the last year, you're in a bad downward spiral." He showed John the flow charts representing the company's financial records for the past four quarters. "Costs are up," he said, pointing to a blue line on the graph. "Profits are down," he said, pointing to the green line. "The profit margins are rapidly shrinking and don't show any sign of improvement. John, we've been friends for a long time, and I hate being the one to tell you this, but maybe you should consider selling."

"It can't be that bad," John said. "We've had slumps before and always pulled out."

"This time's different. It's not just here, either. I'm delivering bad news to all of our small job shop clients. Your business is like so many others. Too small to have the cash resources to weather a long dry spell and, well...", he hesitated. "Given the divorce and buying Doug out, your situation is worse. I don't see much hope for improvement. I think you should sell while you still have something to sell."

Letting John absorb his news for a few moments, Joel stayed quiet and sipped his coffee.

John looked out the window of his office. "I've been in this business twenty-five years. It's my life and I'm not ready to retire. If we work harder…"

Joel cut him off. "No. It's different this time. How many years have you been consistently raising prices? Those days are over. I know the Big Three are requiring significant price reductions from their suppliers and it's not just automotive. All major manufacturing corporations, like Boeing, are doing it. You can't just work harder, raise prices, and have everything work out. You've cut your expenses to the bone. You're a dying breed. It pains me to say that. I know what this business means to you, but the days of the small job shop may be numbered."

"You're right. It's not just the Big Three. Aeroquip asked for price reductions yesterday."

"I hate to use a cliché but these figures don't lie. It's all here in black and white."

John stood up and walked to the window, jamming his hands in his back pockets. "This country was made great, was founded on the small business. I can't believe or I won't believe there's no hope."

"Think you can pay your divorce settlement or Doug with hope?" Joel asked, not unkindly.

"What are other companies doing?"

"They're selling out, going out of business or being taken over. I have one client that was just bought out by their biggest customer. It's the age of the conglomerates."

"The big guys. And leaving the scraps for the rest of us," John said, with anger creeping into his voice.

"That's about the size of it."

"In your opinion, how much time do you think we have?"

"Six or eight months. A year, maybe. On that score, you're better off than a lot of others. The company's debt free." Joel shrugged his shoulders. "You could borrow and that'd keep you afloat longer but I'm not advising that."

"What are the big guys doing that the small companies aren't doing?" John asked.

"A lot of them are playing paper shuffleboard on the stock market but most are throwing their size around, demanding concessions from their suppliers. Japan really scared the hell out of the Big Three and it's just snowballed from there. The small companies aren't big enough to demand concessions from their suppliers and or to refuse their customers' demands."

"It's more than that, Joel," John said. "Competition is good. Our entire economy is based on that fact. You mentioned the Big Three. Look at the quality of American cars. It's dramatically improved. Why? Competition. American manufacturers are making better cars today. While we don't supply the automotive industry, the same principle applies. We have to find a way to get better."

"I'll grant you that. The question is, do you have the time?"

"It's not time. It's know-how I need."

"John, I don't like the way you're thinking. I don't want to see you lose everything. My advice is…"

"Yes, I know what your advice is," John cut him off.

"So what are you going to do?"

"Get better. It's that simple. Get better."

"How?"

"I don't have a clue right now, but I will. There are over forty families depending on ATMI for their livelihoods. I'm not going to let them down."

"John, I've known you too long to doubt your abilities but it's a long shot."

"If I have to choose between rolling over and playing dead or going down swinging, I'll go down swinging."

"It's your business."

For the first time since the meeting began, John smiled.

"Yes, it is my business. Joel, thanks and I'll be in touch." He left Joel to find his own way out of the building.

Twenty minutes later, Randy Tucker, the Operations Manager found John out back of the shop.

"They said you were out here."

"Tuck, things have to change."

"Yeah. I wrote up Ron and Hanson for that fiasco yesterday. It really wasn't Hanson's fault. We'd never trained him on the lathe but he did run a lot of junk that got shipped. I'm going to talk with Quality today and find out who was responsible for final inspection and whoever it was will get written up, too."

"It's more than that. We have to completely rethink what we're doing."

John had no more spoken when a Frisbee went sailing by his head, causing both he and Tuck to duck.

"What the…" Tuck said.

As fast as his short legs would carry him, the beagle dashed after the Frisbee, only catching up to it when it hit the ground. He pawed at the Frisbee.

Jimmy came running around the corner and barely missed running into John.

"Whoa. Hold up there, Jimmy," John said.

"Oh, sorry," Jimmy said. "Dumb dog. Can't even catch a Frisbee."

As the beagle nosed the Frisbee, John said, "How'd you expect him to catch it when he couldn't see it?"

"Huh?"

"It was either out of his line of sight or thrown too hard. There wasn't any way he could catch it. All he could do was chase after it. Do that too many times and he won't chase it at all."

As if on cue, the pup trotted up to John and he bent down, scratching the dog's ears. "Good boy," he said as the dog licked his hand.

"Here, let me show you," John said, walking over to the Frisbee. He picked it up and gently tossed it within the pup's line of sight. The pup dashed after it and leapt into the air, catching it. He trotted back to John and dropped the Frisbee at his feet.

"Mister, that was neat," Jimmy said.

"If we're going to keep meeting like this, you better start calling me John."

Profit pranced around, eager for another go at the Frisbee.

John handed it to Jimmy and said, "Okay, you try it. Make sure he can succeed."

Jimmy tossed the Frisbee and Profit caught it flawlessly.

"That's neat," Jimmy exclaimed. "He can really do it."

"Sure he can and he knows when he's done his job," Tuck said.

John jerked his head toward Tuck.

"What'd you just say?" John asked.

"Uhh, that the dog knows when he's done his job," Tuck answered.

"Of course he does," John said, laughing. "Don't we all know that? Know when we've done our jobs?"

"Sometimes, I guess," Tuck said. "But it's our customers who tell us whether they like it or not. Often after the fact."

"No. Not after the fact. Our customers tell us what they want. That's how we bid the jobs. If we don't have a clear understanding, that's our fault, not theirs. And, we should know every time when we've done our jobs and that goes for everyone in the shop."

"Now, wait a minute, Boss. How many times do customers change things on us?"

"Those are the exceptions that prove the rule. Sure, it happens sometimes, but most of the time, we know exactly what our customers want. And, if we don't, we should."

"What are you driving at?" Tuck asked.

"Jimmy, can I borrow the Frisbee for a second?" John asked.

"Sure." He was feeling very important being involved in an adult conversation.

John took the Frisbee, caught Profit's attention and tossed it. Profit made a mad dash, caught the Frisbee and trotted back to John, dropping the Frisbee at his feet. John bent down and petted the dog.

"See what I mean, Tuck?" John asked, looking up at the Operations Manager.

Tuck cocked his head sideways and said, "What'd you put in your coffee this morning?"

John laughed out loud.

"A big dose of reality, now that you mention it," John said. John scratched Profit behind the ears. "Good dog." He stood up. "This beagle likes to be told he did a good job, but he <u>knows</u> when he's done a good job."

"Okay," Tuck said tentatively.

"Don't you see? We have highly trained machinists. They're good at their jobs. They know what to do as long as we're not throwing Frisbees around a blind corner. Profit doesn't need an inspector to tell him whether he's caught the Frisbee or not."

Tuck looked at John and said, "I think I see what you mean."

"Thank you, Jimmy, and thank you, Profit," John said, petting the pup on the head.

"Tuck, I have to get over to Aeroquip. I want you to rethink the write-up on Hanson. We asked him to do a job when he didn't have the training. Let me know your thoughts when I get back."

3

John pulled into Aeroquip's parking lot, shut off his car and collected his thoughts. He was preparing for the well-deserved verbal thrashing to come. Everyone would get a shot at him; production, quality, engineering and the janitor. After a few moments, he went in and the receptionist told him he'd find Paul Conner, the plant manager, out on the production floor.

Walking through the plant, he was struck with all of the multi-colored graphs and charts on the walls, recording everything from production to scrap to efficiencies. He was used to seeing the safety record up on the wall but this was entirely new. Aeroquip had always kept information private yet here it was posted for everyone to see. The atmosphere was different, too. Aeroquip had always had a tense feel to it; a company where cannibalism was okay. Yet, people seemed generally more relaxed. It had been nearly a year since John had been on the plant floor. There had been no reason to visit until yesterday but 1,000 bad parts certainly was enough reason although it was the worst possible reason John could imagine.

Lost in thought, John didn't hear Paul approach until he clapped him on the shoulder.

"Good morning, John. I appreciate your stopping by," Paul said.

"Stopping by?" John thought. Now he knew he was at an entirely different company from the Aeroquip he'd always known.

"Paul, I am sorry about the bad shipment. We'll have the replacements here by end of work today. There's no excuse. We just blew it," John said sincerely.

"Have you figured out what went wrong?" Paul asked.

"Yes."

"Have you figured out how to keep it from happening again?" Paul asked.

Thunderstruck, John just looked at Paul.

"Where did the process break down? What can we do to help?" Paul asked.

"Tuck's on top of it. He found who was at fault and…"

"Not person. Process," Paul said.

"Process? The procedures are fine. We just blew it," John said, wondering where this conversation was heading.

"If the process was fine, we wouldn't have received a bad shipment," Paul said. "You need to Poke-yoke it."

"I need to what it?" John asked, raising his eyebrows.

"Poke-yoke. It means to error-proof. Let me show you what I mean," Paul said and led John over to a work area. "In this process, the parts are washed between steps two and three, so when an operator would finish with step two, he'd drop the parts in the wash and when the next operator was ready for them, he'd take them out of the wash. We were continually getting rejects on this part until we discovered that the amount of time the parts stayed in the wash was crucial." He pointed to a laminated sheet on the machine. "See? The parts can only stay in the wash between four and seven minutes. Any shorter or longer, and they're scrap. So the window of four to seven minutes is now part of the process."

"That solved the problem?" John asked.

"No. The solution came with our cell design and a timing light. Now, one operator is doing the entire operation. After four minutes of being in the wash, the timing light is green. At six minutes, the timing light is yellow and at seven, it's red. It's all part of our one process flow."

"Bet your operator loved having a second job to do," John said.

Paul smiled. "Yes, at first, it was a challenge until the operator realized the benefits to him."

"To him?"

"Sure. He controls what happens in his work area. He doesn't have to worry about someone else dropping parts in the wash when he's not looking. It reduced his stress immensely and improved our quality. It's improved our cycle times as well. The timing light was his idea," Paul said.

As they were standing there, the green light switched to yellow. The operator took the parts out of the wash and prepared them for the next step.

"It's a visual cue for the operator," Paul said.

"Like a stoplight," John said.

"Yes. The operator actually got the idea from the Kan-ban system. It was a great adaptation."

"Paul, why are you suddenly speaking Greek?" John asked. "You've used several words that I have no idea what they mean."

"I'm sorry. We try to stay away from that. But, it is a new way of doing things and language is part of it."

"New way?" John asked, very curious.

"Lean Manufacturing."

"You put Aeroquip on a diet?" John asked.

"In a manner of speaking, yes."

As Paul spoke, the red light came on.

The operator withdrew the parts and threw them in a bin marked Scrap.

"Paul, he just threw away parts," John said, incredulous.

"Sure. They're scrap. He knows it. We all know it, so we get rid of it rather than risk having bad parts slip through."

"Why doesn't he send them to the rework department?" John asked.

"We haven't had a rework department since going Lean," Paul said.

"No rework department? No wonder you want price concessions. Your costs must be skyrocketing, throwing away parts like that," John said.

"Just the opposite. Our costs are down."

"Sure," John thought, *"You're squeezing your suppliers like me,"* but he didn't say a word.

"Speaking of price concessions, we need to take a look at that," Paul said. I called Larry Myers yesterday."

"Yes, I know. He's looking into it, but I just don't see how we can do it."

"I think you can. You just need to get Lean," Paul said.

"That's one way I could meet your price concessions. I'll stop eating. That'll get me Lean," John said.

"Here's some good news," Paul said. "I want you to take a look at a new part that you might be able to handle."

"If it's machining, we can handle it," John said, a bit defensive.

"The question is if it's one of your core competencies."

"Paul, I've been supplying Aeroquip for how many years? Whenever you had a difficult part, I was always the first person you'd call. Don't tell me that one bad shipment eroded your confidence in me," John said.

"Oh, no. Not at all. That's exactly why I'm asking you first. Come on. Let's go to my office and you can see the prototype and specs," Paul said.

As they walked through the plant to Paul's office, John's mind was reeling. John was mentally kicking himself for the bad shipment and for not seeing Paul on a more regular basis. He needed the new work, especially now. So much had changed at Aeroquip that it was like an entirely new company and Paul was throwing questions at him that he couldn't readily answer. The entire plant lay-out was different. Even the people were different. The 'work cells', as Paul had called them, were really like small little factories within one large facility. There wasn't the normal confusion that was present in plants. It reminded John of a neighborhood. Each work group seemed self-contained yet they all relied on the plant for basic services, just like homes in a sub-division rely on the city for street maintenance and other commonly-used services.

When they reached Paul's office, the new part prototype was on his desk. Paul picked it up and handed it to John. It was steel coupling with four openings and weighed about four pounds. It was a larger part than he normally produced but he knew they could produce it. Depending on how many parts Aeroquip wanted, John knew he could jerryrig a couple of his machines to produce it. He'd have to invest in some larger bits for the borings but he could do that. He was in no position to turn down business.

"What do you think?" Paul asked.

"We can do this," John said.

"Let's talk about that. Do you have time for lunch?"

"Sure."

"Where would you like to go? What are you hungry for?" Paul asked.

"Anything's fine."

"No. Tell me what you'd really like to eat for lunch."

John thought for a moment then said, "A steak. I could use a nice, thick juicy steak today."

"Great. Okay. Now, should we go to Vegetarian Palace or Sam's Steak House?"

John laughed out loud.

"Paul, you know as well as I do that Sam's Steak House has the best steaks in the county. I doubt that the Vegetarian Palace even has sirloin on its menu."

"Good choice."

4

After they'd ordered, Paul said, "What do you think of the part?"

"We can do it," John answered.

"Now, back to my earlier question. Is it one of your core competencies?"

"Paul, I have to be frank with you. I don't know what you mean by that phrase."

"I appreciate your honesty. That's why I asked you what you wanted for lunch and where you wanted to go. No one does steak better than Sam's Steak House. You can get a steak lots of other places but steaks are one of Sam's core competencies. This restaurant is set up to prepare and serve the best steaks around and you know he's making a profit. Everything in this place is designed to do exactly that. That's a core competency. It's all part of the Lean process. Lean manufacturing is the future."

The waitress interrupted their conversation and served their meals to them.

Paul waited until John had taken two bites of his steak before continuing.

"Steak knives are already at every place setting. The steaks are served on metal plates on wooden service trays because wood doesn't conduct heat and they reduce the risk of customers getting inadvertently burned." He picked up the wire rack of condiments. "Several choices of steak sauce are already here so you don't have to ask the waitress for them. And, you know their open-flame grills are fired up at the right temperatures for steaks. The wait staff is fully versed in the steaks they offer, from sirloin to porterhouse, and even special meats, like Black Angus steaks. Now, if you wanted fish, I doubt if the waitress would know the difference between a Halibut and Sea Bass."

"There isn't even fish on the menu," John protested.

"That's my point exactly. This place is a good…no, it's a great example of Lean manufacturing and core competencies are a key element."

"Paul, Aeroquip is an important customer to us. We'll do what it takes to keep your business," John said.

"I know that. You're on our A list of suppliers. Aeroquip's at the point in our conversion to Lean where we're bringing our suppliers on board. That is, our good suppliers, the ones we want to build stronger relationships with. John, we have a good business relationship and I like to think we're friends. I'm not telling you that ATMI has to go to Lean Manufacturing but what I am telling you is that Aeroquip is committed a hundred percent to doing business with the Lean philosophy."

John buttered a roll, considering his next words very carefully.

"Paul, I don't know what more I can tell you other than we'll do what it takes to keep Aeroquip's business." He pondered how much he should reveal to him and decided to be more open than he normally would. "You know what the economy's like. Everybody's scrambling for business. On top of that, I'm buying out Doug and…well, there's just no other way to say this, my divorce is going to be expensive. ATMI is financially solid and we'll weather these storms and, frankly, I'm looking for the best way to keep ATMI financially strong and solid. New business is crucial to that."

"I'm sorry about your divorce. I know mine cost me a bundle," Paul said, smiling sympathetically. "I agree that new business is vital to any company but it's the right new business that's crucial. Northside Manufacturing just went belly-up and they had over three million dollars in incoming business but they just couldn't deliver the product at a profit to them. I hate to admit this but Aeroquip may have played a part in their failure. We hit them pretty hard with our demands in quality, quantity and cost cuts. Now, we weren't the only ones but…" his voice trailed off.

"That wasn't your fault, Paul. You've used this restaurant as an example. Let me do the same. Imagine if you told Sam you'd only pay fifty percent of what the menu said. Think he'd serve you a steak?"

"That's the rub. Add another element. What if I told Sam I'd pay him fifty percent of the price and guaranteed I'd keep his restaurant at seventy-five percent capacity, he might be tempted. But, unless there's a fifty percent profit margin in these steaks, he'd be out of business shortly. That's what happened to Northside."

"I see your point," John said.

"You said you'd do what it takes to keep Aeroquip as a customer. First off, you're not in jeopardy of losing our business. What I'm going to suggest, strongly suggest, is that you convert ATMI to Lean manufacturing."

"You've used that term before and I'm clueless. I hear about all of the latest, hottest fads and for what? The tweak of the week? I've built ATMI on solid business practices and that's what I'm going to continue doing."

"I couldn't agree more. Lean manufacturing is world-class, state-of-the-art business practice in manufacturing. It's not a passing fad. And, I'll tell you this, companies that don't go Lean aren't going to be around. It's that simple. The

Lean process is such a revolution, it's like introducing cars to a horse-based transportation culture."

"Paul, that kind of thing may work for a big company like Aeroquip or the Big Three but we're a small job shop," he protested.

"Aeroquip is just a larger job shop, when you stop to think about it. You have to learn to adapt. Lean will work for you."

John looked at him skeptically.

"I don't blame you for having doubts. Believe me, if I hadn't been forced into it, I wouldn't have done it," Paul said.

"Who forced you?"

"Our CEO. In retrospect, the man's a visionary. However, when I first heard about Lean, I thought he'd been eating too many funny mushrooms."

John chuckled at that statement.

"It's all based on the Toyoto Production System…"

"Let me stop you right there. It may be politically incorrect but just because something is Japanese doesn't make it good. I have nothing against the Japanese…"

"John, the Japanese came within a whisker of burying the American automotive business."

"With unfair trade agreements, stiff tariffs…"

"All that played a part, no doubt, but the fact is that American consumers bought Japanese cars because they were better made. Better quality and cheaper. The Big Three couldn't compete. American automotive manufacturers learned and they learned fast. Funny thing is that the guru was Dr. Edward Deming, an American. After the second World War, we were fat, dumb and happy, and didn't listen to his ideas, but Japan did. What's happened is that a whole new philosophy of business has emerged. It is a philosophy, too. Understanding that is important. Above and beyond that, the absolute most important key is commitment. If our CEO hadn't been committed and driven Lean through all of our plants, it wouldn't have happened. It won't happen at ATMI if you aren't committed, either."

"How can I be committed when I don't even know what it is?" John asked, clearly exasperated.

"John, in spite of the confusing Japanese terms, this isn't rocket science. It's really very simple. Lean manufacturing is about one thing. How to eliminate waste. Waste that comes from things like overproduction, costly inventory, unproductive time waiting around, unnecessary movement of parts, material and tooling around the plant, overprocessing, and of course, scrap. These are things that slow down your production, hurt quality and add to your operating costs. Not to mention requiring 'apology' visits to your customers, like this one." Paul smiled.

"Paul, you seem really fired up about Lean manufacturing."

"I am. However, at first, I was skeptical and dug in my heels."

"What turned you around?"

"The results. We watched our quality go up, efficiencies climb, scrap go down, increased profits and decreased costs, not to mention an incredible reduction in stress."

"I noticed that at the plant. The atmosphere is very different, much more relaxed. So, the numbers convinced you."

Paul took a sip of water. He was clearly reflecting on his answer. "No. I can't say that. While the numbers were convincing, it was the change in our employees."

"How so?"

"Again, remember not only was I resistant, but so was everyone in the plant. The Lean process was driven by the CEO. In the old days, the operators clocked their time, running machines, and depending on the inspectors to tell them if they'd done good work or not. When you stop to think about it, that alone is really demoralizing. How many times have your machinists gotten upset because they thought they produced a good part only to have an inspector reject it?"

"All the time."

"Or, the reverse. An inspector insists that parts be shipped when the machinists think they're junk?"

"That happens, too," John said.

"With Lean, our operators know when they've produced a good part. They scrap the junk and they know when they've done a good job. Morale skyrocketed. I have to admit we did have some turnover. The employees who didn't want that kind of responsibility or accountability, the ones who just wanted to clock their time and as well as the chronic complainers, did leave. But, those that stayed, they're really motivated and have more pride in their work than I ever thought possible."

"Know when they've done a good job," John mused, more to himself than to Paul.

"I mentioned that we were at the stage of beginning to involve our suppliers in the process. Our goal is to improve our working relationship with our suppliers. We're holding a week-long seminar on Lean next week. Actually, it's for some of our other plants that haven't come on line yet, but I'd like you to attend. I know it's awfully short notice. We weren't planning on inviting suppliers for a few months."

"A week-long program. I don't know if I can take that kind of time away from the job."

"John, the question is can you afford not to take that kind of time? You'll get a jump on every other supplier Aeroquip has if you start now. Bring Tuck along, too. You'll need support implementing Lean."

"That's a big time commitment," John said.

"Isn't that something, though? It's sad to think that ATMI would be in serious trouble if both you and Tuck were gone for a week, isn't it? Wouldn't it be great if your employees knew what was good work or not, on their own?"

"Know when they were successful," John said.

"Yes."

"Okay. I'll be there and I'll bring Tuck." John suddenly became very animated. "This may be exactly what I was looking for. My CPA said, just this morning, that we couldn't work harder but had to work smarter. I know how bright and talented our employees are and I have not been capitalizing on that. I just taught that lesson to a little boy this morning when I should've been teaching it to myself."

The waitress appeared, placed the check on the table and began clearing away their dishes. John glanced down at the steak bones left on both his and Paul's plates.

"Would you please put the bones in a doggy bag?" he asked.

"Sure," she said, taking the plates away.

"I didn't know you had a dog," Paul said.

"I don't but there's this kid, Jimmy, who's been around the shop the last couple of days. He must live in the neighborhood. Anyway, he has this beagle. Damnedest dog you've ever seen, and, get this, the dog's name is Profit."

"Profit?" Paul asked, laughing.

"Profit. There's a funny story that involves Aeroquip. I was out back, watching the Aeroquip shipment of rejected parts being unloaded and I hear Jimmy calling Profit. 'Here, Profit. Where are you? Where'd you go?' And, I was wondering exactly the same thing, where did our profit go? In a few minutes, his Profit showed up and if what you're saying is true, you've shown me where to find my profit," John said. "Anyway, the doggy bag is for Profit. I think he'd like a nice steak bone."

Just as John reached for the check, Paul snatched it.

"Now, wait a minute," John said. "I'll get that."

"No. Since you're willing to take a chance and come to the seminar next week, you've given me the gift of a supplier who's going to launch continuous improvements at his shop. Besides, I'll get to use you as a Guinea pig and learn from your reactions how to improve our future supplier seminars."

"Well…"

"I insist," Paul said.

"Thank you."

"Just remember what I said about commitment. You will have to be the driving force to get Lean implemented. It will not work otherwise. Remember the old saying, 'You can't jump a canyon in two leaps.'"

5

When John got back to ATMI, he didn't park in front as he normally did but parked on the side of the building. Retrieving the doggy bag, he got out of his car and went around to the back of the shop.

Outside the back door were three employees, apparently just talking. When they spotted John walking toward them, they began nervously milling around. Hank Zepper threw down a lit cigarette and ground it out with the heel of his boot.

"What's up, guys?" John asked as he approached the men.

"Nothing," Carter Alson said. "Just taking a break."

John glanced at his watch and said, "You're taking a break now?"

"Why not?" Hank said, jutting out his jaw. "Yeah, I know it's not our normally scheduled break time but I don't have any work to do. So, what am I supposed to do? Just stand around and wait until Craig gets off his butt and gives me my next job?"

"What about you two?" John asked the other men.

"Same here," Carter said.

"Me, too, I guess," Roy Banks said, but he seemed less sure of his answer than either Carter or Hank.

"Let me get this straight. None of you have any work to do? Craig hasn't assigned anything for you to do?" John said.

"You got it," Hank said. Hank always had a chip on his shoulder the size of Colorado and now was no exception.

Roy glanced down, shuffled a foot and said, "Yeah, well, I suppose I could be cleaning some parts but I'll have plenty of time to do that before my shift ends."

"How long have you been out here?" John asked.

"Not long. Just a few minutes," Carter said.

"Please tell me the truth. You won't get in trouble," John coaxed.

"Okay," Hank said. "I haven't had anything to do for the last hour. These two have been out here with me all that time, too."

John's mental calculator was humming, counting the wasted money he was paying three employees who didn't have any work.

"Did any of you let Craig know you didn't have any work?" John asked.

"No. That's not my job," Hank said. "Craig knows the work load and should be keeping me busy so I wouldn't have to stand around cooling my heels."

"But, you didn't tell him," John pressed.

"Like I said. Not my job. I run the Bridgeport and Craig's got ears. He can hear when that machine stops. It means I'm out of work."

John bristled at the answers he was receiving but bit his tongue. Paul's words were ringing in his ears. *"Talk about waste,"* he thought.

After a few moments of uncomfortable silence, John said to Carter and Roy, "Why don't you two go on back to work. I want to talk with Hank privately."

Relieved for themselves, Carter and Roy headed back into the shop, leaving Hank to face John alone.

"I'm going to get a butt-chewing," Hank said, as he flushed red.

"No, you're not. I appreciate your honesty and really need you to be honest now. How often does this kind of thing go on?"

"I don't hold nothing back. I'll tell you like it is. It happens all the time."

"Take a walk with me," John said, heading toward the field in back of the shop.

"You're sure you're not taking me to the horse shed for a whipping?" Hank asked, laughing nervously.

"No. I couldn't give you a whipping if I tried. You've got six inches and fifty pounds on me," John said as he led the way.

When they reached the field, John sat down on a large rock. Hank leaned against the fence, withdrew a cigarette from the pack in his shirt pocket. He took a couple of drags on the cigarette, waiting for John to get to the point.

"Hank, how long have you worked here?"

"Ten years. If you're thinking of firing me, just get it over with. I told Craig when he threatened to fire my ass that I'd have a job within a day and if he ever threatened me again, he wouldn't have to worry about carrying it out. I'd quit," Hank said.

Taken aback, John just looked at Hank.

"Hell, John, I've got a journeyman's card. How long do you think I'd be out of work?"

"Hold up. I'm not firing you. I'm after information. Just relax, will you? You're one of the best machinists we have. You can make the Bridgeport sing. Why on earth would I want to fire you?"

Hank didn't answer.

"Hank, I need your help."

"Oh, here it comes," Hank interrupted. "The old one-for-all and all-for-one speech. That's a little hard to swallow when I'm cramming down my lunch in twenty minutes and you're dining on steak at Sam's Steak House," he said pointing at the doggy bag sill clutched in John's hand.

John looked at the bag and placed it on the ground beside him.

"I was having lunch with Paul from Aeroquip, but where I was having lunch isn't the point. You know we shipped 1,000 bad parts to them yesterday."

"I heard about it, but that was first shift, not second. Damned inspectors didn't do their jobs."

"Is it the inspectors' jobs?" John asked.

"Hell, yes. Nobody listens to the machinists. The supervisors don't listen to us but they listen to the inspectors and some of the inspectors have never even run a machine."

"But don't you know when you've produced a good part?" John asked.

"I do. At least, I do in my opinion, but the inspectors will override me. I've had them change the controls on the machine and really screw things up. I try to tell them but they won't listen. The worst is when I know it's junk but they ship it anyway. And, when the parts get rejected, who gets written up? It's not the inspectors or the supervisor. It's the operator. That's bullcrap and I've said it before."

John knew with unerring certainty that Hank was right. Again, Paul's words came back to him. Waste. In this case, not only waste of time and talent, but waste of knowledge. Hank knew the Bridgeport better than anybody in the shop and he could produce good parts. Yet, people weren't listening to him.

"What would you do to make it better?" John asked.

"Hell, start listening to people."

"How would you feel about the responsibility that went along with making those calls?"

"It'd be a damn sight better than what's going on now. I get my butt chewed when I try to tell someone the parts are bad. Then, I get chewed again when the parts get rejected. If I was calling the shots, I wouldn't be shipping junk. I'd take that responsibility in a heart beat."

John just listened as Hank really began getting fired up.

"Since you've asked, it's also crap that parts come to me and they're a mess. Some people just don't give a rat's…hind end. They run their machines without even thinking about what they're doing. They push the parts down the line to me and they're junk. I do what I can to fix them, then Craig jumps me because I'm taking too long."

"If things are that bad, why do you stay here?" John asked with genuine interest.

"You think ATMI is any different from any other place? It's the same all over. My brother works for Snyder's and his supervisor with an engineering degree who couldn't tell metric from English threading. At least Craig can run a machine. Not as good as me but he's gotten his hands dirty," Hank said. "When you get right down to it, I stay here because of you. I respect you. But, I don't see you as much as in the old days."

"The old days," John thought. The good, ole days when ATMI raised their prices every year or charged time and materials. It was hard not to make money then.

"Yes. I miss those days, too, but they're long gone. We have to find ways to improve," John said. "We have to cut out the waste."

Neither John nor Hank heard Craig Green approach.

"No wonder we're running behind," Craig said. "John, if you'd quit disturbing the employees, we might get some work done," he said, laughing.

John ignored Craig's attempt at humor.

"We've been discussing some things," John said. "Hank, thanks for taking the time to talk with me. I appreciate your insights."

"No problem," Hank said, then he and Craig walked back to the shop.

"Waste, waste, waste," John said when they were out of ear shot, mulling over what Hank had told him. He saw some movement at the edge of the woods and looked over as Profit came barreling out of the woods, in hot pursuit of a rabbit. When the rabbit zigged, Profit zagged. They cut a fast Z path across the field, the rabbit finally outsmarting the young and inexperienced pup when it disappeared down a hole. Profit slid to a stop, looked around, sniffed the air, and howled.

John heard Jimmy calling Profit a few seconds before he came running out of the woods.

Jimmy waved at John and ran up to him, out of breath. Profit made a beeline for them, wagging his tail when he reached them.

"Did you see that?" Jimmy said. "He almost had that rabbit. He's going to be a good hunter."

John knew that the rabbit was never in any real danger from the inexperienced pup but the kid had a right to be proud of his dog. He could be a fine hunter some day.

Profit began nosing around the paper bag beside John.

"Oh, here," John said, reaching down for the bag. "I got these for Profit."

"Wow, thanks," Jimmy said.

John handed the T-bone to Profit who eagerly took it and began gnawing on it.

After chewing on it for a few seconds, he dropped it and licked John's fingers before nosing at the paper bag again.

"Oh, no, you don't," John said, laughing. "One bone right now is plenty. If I give you this other one now, you'll just waste one of them."

"Sorry. He's being greedy," Jimmy said.

"That's just nature or instinct, Jimmy," John said. "He doesn't know when he's going to get another bone so he'll grab as many as he can right now."

"But, I feed him every day," Jimmy protested, seeming hurt by John's words.

"Of course you do. I just meant he'd horde the bones. Bury one of them until later."

"Yeah, he does that all the time but I think he forgets where he buries them," Jimmy said. "Mom found three bones in her rose garden. He'll steal the cat's food even when his dish is full. Well, he did until Whiskers smacked him on the nose. Then, he learned."

"There's a lot of that going around right now," John said.

"Huh?"

"Nothing. I just mean we're all learning lessons and getting smacked on the nose," John said.

Jimmy only looked confused in response.

"He's a pup. He's supposed to be learning new lessons." John reached down and petted the pup on the head. "Thank God even old dogs can learn new tricks," he said.

6

As John walked back into the shop, he heard two employees arguing and he went to their area to find out what was going on.

"Hey, John," Zack said. "I'm glad you're here. I need your help."

"What's up?"

Zack's body was tense and John saw he was clenching and unclenching his fists. Zack had a temper but he'd never seen him strike a blow. However, right now, he looked like he could at any minute.

"Mike, the 'newby' who's been here all of three months, is telling me we should be setting this job up in under thirty minutes. It ain't gonna happen. I've been setting this job up for a year and I know it takes a good two hours."

"Calm down, Zack. Don't blow a fuse," John said.

"John, I worked on this type of machine before at Tri-Star and I know it can be done," Mike Marston said.

Tri-Star was a Tier One automotive supplier and one of the largest machining companies in the country.

If Mike was right, what was Tri-Star doing that ATMI wasn't?

Zack's ego was on the line and John had to tread very carefully.

"Mike, I know you have good experience from Tri-Star but we're not making automotive parts. We're making invasive medical devices and I'm guessing that our specs. are a lot tougher here. This isn't a dashboard you're making but a shunt for kidney dialysis. Not to mention our aerospace parts."

"We worked to one thousandth tolerances," Mike said.

One thousandth, John thought. That's what ATMI had to meet.

"Not only that, John," Zack said, "But he's trying to get us to change the whole process."

"That's not correct," Mike said. "I looked for the process sheets for this job and couldn't find one. I asked around and apparently people change things, do what they have to do, to make it work. I thought it was okay to make suggestions."

"What the hell do I need process sheets for?" Zack shouted. "I've been doing this job for over a year!"

Mike turned toward Zack and said, "What happens if you're not here?"

"Good question," John thought.

"I am here," Zack said, "So what's the big deal?"

"Okay, okay," John said. "We'll get to the bottom of this. Mike, we're on a tight schedule so let's get the job set up the way we've always done it so we can make our shipping deadline but I am interested in your ideas of how we can minimize set-up times. These parts have to ship by Friday."

"You call that fast? A tight deadline?" Mike asked. "I produced oil pans that were on cars within twelve hours. That's fast."

"That's stupid," Zack said. "If Tri-Star was so damned good, how come they were working on that kind of tight deadline?"

"It's called Just In Time or JIT, you moron," Mike said.

"Why, you little…" Zack said.

"Whoa. Stop it right now," John interceded. "Zack, you set up this job and get it running. Mike, you come with me."

"Sure thing, boss," Zack said, gloating over his victory.

When they'd walked out of ear shot of Zack, John said, "Mike, it sounds like you have some good ideas and I want to hear them. There are a couple of differences you'll have to keep in mind. We're not an automotive supplier and we're not a big company. We're a small job shop. Things are different here."

Chagrined, Mike kept silent as he walked beside John.

Unable to keep quiet any longer, Mike said, "Can I speak freely?"

"Of course," John said. "The only requirement is maintaining respect for everyone."

"Calling him a moron wasn't respectful. Sorry."

"No. Anyway, what did you want to say?"

"I don't think being a small job shop makes you any different from a big automotive supplier."

"It does make a difference."

"That's your paradigm," Mike said.

"My what?" John asked.

"Paradigm. What you believe is a paradigm. Before Christopher Columbus, people thought the earth was flat. That was their paradigm," Mike said.

John immediately understood why Zack could get so hot under the collar working with Mike.

"A paradigm is a myth?" John asked.

"No. Not a myth but a set of beliefs. You do something one way for years and when someone tries to tell you a better way, a faster way, you automatically assume it's wrong because it conflicts with your experience or your paradigm. You don't even bother to try it out."

"This company is very successful so we're doing a lot of things right," John said.

"You said I could speak freely," Mike said.

"I do want you to speak freely but remember you have your own paradigms, don't you?"

"Well, yeah."

"Your experience is at a big company and an automotive supplier so your beliefs were established there, right?"

"Yes."

"In a job shop, our volumes are low and our customer demand is unpredictable. Automotive is a high volume industry," John said. "Those two elements make a big difference."

"I don't see how."

"How many parts did your plant at Tri-Star produce?"

"A couple dozen," Mike said.

"We produce over five thousand different parts," John said.

"How many different parts will you produce in one day?" Mike asked.

"Just one part. One job may run for three or four days without any set-up changes," John said.

"I produced an average of ten different parts every day. My personal record is five parts. That meant five different set-ups within one shift," Mike said.

"What the..." John asked but cut himself off. John immediately realized that the real question was 'how', or better yet, 'why'.

"I'm not sure I understand. You'd produce five different parts in a day and produce the same five parts the next day?"

"Yes."

"Why? Why not produce all of the one part before going on to the next?" John asked.

"Customer demand," Mike said. "Let me tell you what would happen. When I got to work, I'd check the computer and find out what I had to produce that day. Our trucks left every two hours and the schedule showed which parts had to be on which trucks. So, the first part might be an oil pan for an SUV and the second part might be an oil pan for sedan. It's all part of JIT. Tri-Star had to get good at rapid set-ups or we'd lose the business."

"That sounds like mass confusion to me," John said.

"It was at first until we went to cells. You know, one piece flow."

John rubbed his forehead. He was beginning to get a headache.

"Mike, I want to learn more about what you know but not right now. How familiar are you with the lathe operations?"

"Not at all."

"Okay. Come with me." He and Mike walked over to the lathes and told the operator to start teaching Mike about the lathes and to have Mike spend the rest of his shift with him.

Looking around the shop, John found Tuck deburring a component.

"Hey, Tuck, we need to talk."

"Can it wait a few minutes? I have to get these parts for Textrax. Oh, by the way, we're going to lose money on these parts, too, because you decided to do a favor for them."

"What happened?" John said, sighing. "They called and only needed five pieces of this component. I checked the inventory listing which showed six pieces completed and in stock, so I agreed to deliver them tomorrow. But, since they were in inventory, Textrax started negotiating with me on price and I agreed to $25.00. I know they normally sell for $100.00 but they were just sitting in inventory and we don't know how much longer they'll even be buying this component so I thought we'd make some quick cash. So, what's the problem?"

Tuck looked at John and said, "I went to inventory but there were only five pieces, not six. One piece is tagged 'thread undersize by one-tenth' and another piece is tagged 'hex oversize two thousandths, can be reworked,' which means we only had three good pieces. I'm having Jonas rework one of the pieces but the other one was hopeless so I'm making a new one. Instead of a quick $125.00, this favor for Textrax is costing us."

John grimaced hearing what Tuck told him.

"Tuck, you're doing the right thing," John said. "When you get done, track me down."

As John headed for his office, he passed the milling area and stopped to watch for a few minutes.

Harry waved at John and said, "Thought I'd do a little catch-up, John."

"Catch-up?" John said with specter of another late shipment to a client flooding his already aching head. "Why are we late on this job?"

"We're not late. In fact, we don't even have an order at all, but they order this part every month. I had some spare time so I thought I'd run a few more and put them in inventory so we're ahead of the game when they do call."

John knew that it wasn't uncommon for them to be running parts when they didn't have orders but it was normally a supervisor assigning the work to an employee who didn't have anything to do. It was great to see an employee with initiative. But the question haunting John now was if the initiative was being properly directed.

"Harry, I really like your initiative. Thank you. We always need to be finding ways of working smarter and your attitude is a great help," John said, heading for his office.

By this time, his headache was close to pounding. He stopped at the kitchenette, grabbed a couple of aspirin and downed them with a glass of water.

While waiting for Tuck, he stayed in his office and began sorting through the stack of telephone messages that had accumulated in his absence. Seventeen messages and he was only gone a few hours. How could he manage to be out of here for a week? How could he take the time? What was it Paul had said? How could he afford not to take the time. Yes, that was what Paul had said.

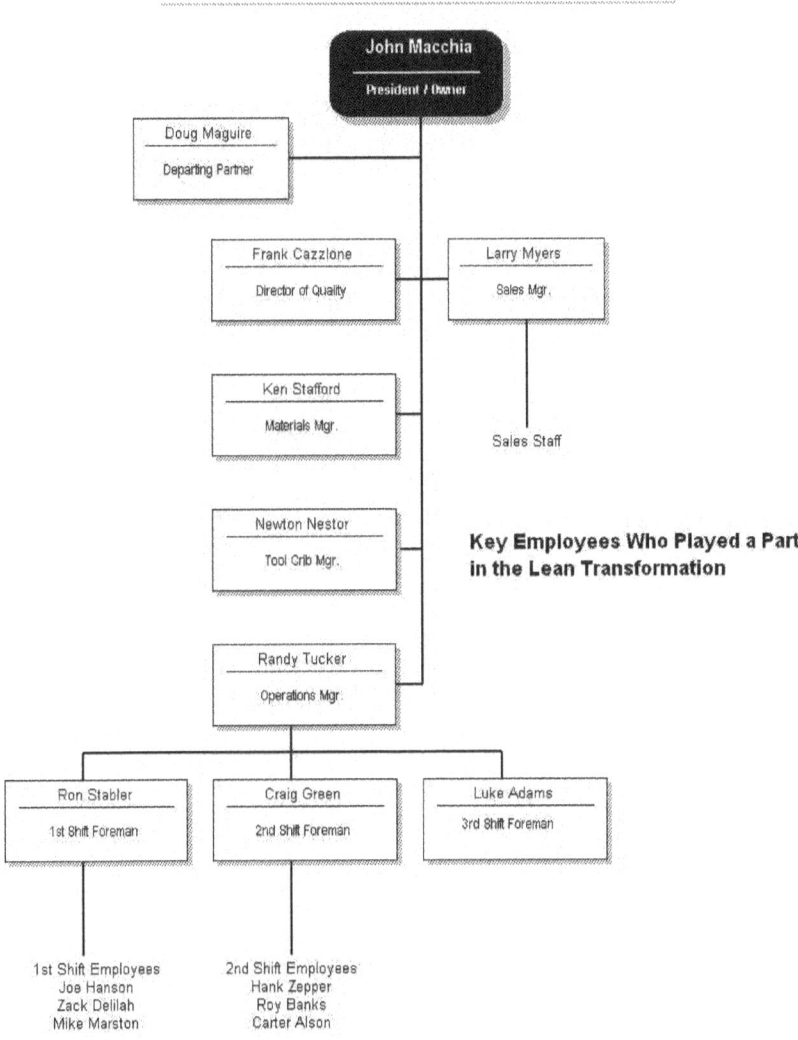

ATMI Organization Chart

Key Employees Who Played a Part
in the Lean Transformation

7

When Tuck came into John's office, John asked him to close the door as he was getting up from his desk. He walked to the small conference table in the corner and sat down. Tuck sat down across from him.

"Did you get the parts done for Textrax?"

"Yes, and they've already been shipped."

"Good. Clear your schedule next week. We're going to a seminar."

"Which day?"

"The entire week," John said, waiting for the inevitable explosion.

"No way. There's no way I can go to a seminar for a whole week. Both of us out of here for an entire week? There's too much to do," Tuck said, vehemently shaking his head.

"Yes, we are going and for the entire week," John said in a tone that made it abundantly clear they were going.

"What on God's green earth is so important that you'd take both of us out of here for an entire week?"

"The future of ATMI," John simply said.

Taken aback, Tuck looked at John, his face a combination of surprise and consternation.

"What are you telling me, John? Are we in serious trouble?"

"No. We're not going to be, either, if I have anything to say about it and since it's my company, I do."

"What brought this on?"

"The last two days have been a rude awakening. If we don't do something different than what we've done in the past, we don't have much of a future. Tuck, I met with Joel, the CPA, yesterday and, this is in strictest confidence, he suggested that I sell ATMI while there was still time. Our profit margins show a steady decline for the last four quarters. It's serious."

Tuck was speechless.

John waited him out.

"We've been through tough times before," Tuck said, "We'll get through this."

"That's the whole point. It's not just us. It's the way some companies are doing business that's killing them. Joel said that all the small job shops were in serious trouble and he called me a dying breed yesterday. As Mark Twain said, 'The reports of my demise are greatly exaggerated.'"

"So your answer is to go to a seminar?"

"No, that was a gift from Paul Conner at Aeroquip. They're hosting this seminar for some of their other plants and are going to be holding seminars for their suppliers in a couple of months but Paul invited us to attend next week's so we're going."

"What's the topic?"

"Lean manufacturing."

"Another flavor of the month," Tuck said sarcastically.

"I don't think so. What do you know about Lean?"

"Not much. Nothing really, but I do know we know how to run our business and I can't see how people from the outside have answers we don't have."

"Lean manufacturing is all about eliminating waste."

"They're going to spend a week telling us how to cut our scrap rate?" Tuck asked.

"It's a lot more than that. It's an entire philosophy. I'm not saying we're going to adopt Lean manufacturing but given the waste I've seen here in the last two days, I'm going to go and listen. So are you."

"What waste?" Tuck asked, with an edge to his voice. As Operations Manager, keeping scrap and waste down to a minimum was his responsibility and he thought they were doing a good job.

John raised his hands and said, "Don't over-react. This isn't an attack on you or what you've been doing. It's a chance to take a look at an entirely new way of doing things."

"Again, what waste?" Tuck persisted.

"All right. Let me run through the list. First, we have the bad shipment to Aeroquip. How many parts? Fifty? There's not enough profit in that job to cover that kind of mistake. That's a waste. Second, when I got back from Aeroquip, I found three employees out back, standing around talking and they'd been there for at least an hour because they didn't have any work to do. Third, walking through the shop today, Mike and Zack almost came to blows, arguing over set-up times—"

"People argue here all the time. It's normally about how to best do the job. I don't think you can call that waste," Tuck said, interrupting John.

"It is waste when Zack was absolutely opposed to listening to any new ideas. When our company culture is closed and we don't even give new ideas a chance, we're signing our own death warrant. It is a waste. Four, Harry was running parts without an order—"

Interrupting John again, Tuck said, "Now hold up a second. We do that all the time. We know what parts are going to be ordered and it gives us a head start. How can that possibly be waste?"

"What if they don't ever buy those parts?"

"But, they always have…"

"Number four is storing those parts. That costs us. I'm afraid to find out how bad of shape our inventory is in, stockpiling parts that we may or may not sell."

"Our inventory's fine. Yeah, there was a mix-up on the Textrax components but what makes you think there are other errors?"

"What makes you think there aren't other errors?"

"We have so much in inventory there are bound to be mistakes, but we normally have enough to cover short-runs and emergencies."

"Tuck, that's like buying two gallons of milk for one bowl of cereal. By the time you need the rest of the milk, it's soured."

"Unless it's a really big bowl of cereal," Tuck said and he laughed. "I mean we are forty miles from the cereal capital of the world."

"If you're thinking of buying enough milk for General Foods and Kellogg's, it'll take more than two gallons," John said, laughing. "Okay, let me give you another example. When you buy gas for your car, you fill the tank, but you don't store a hundred filled gas cans in your garage. Same principle."

"I see your point but that doesn't mean I agree."

"Fair enough. I don't understand Lean manufacturing but it's something we're going to investigate. Paul thinks it's the best thing since Michael Jordon picked up a basketball. He says Aeroquip's efficiencies are skyrocketing, costs are down, quality and productivity are up, and their profits are increasing."

"He shared that with you? Keep-it-close-to-the-vest Paul?" Tuck asked.

"Not just with me. They have their performance records plastered all over the plant. Every employee can take a look and see how well the company is doing."

"You're kidding."

"Aeroquip is a hundred percent committed to Lean manufacturing. Paul really stressed that point, too. He said that absolute, unequivocal commitment from the top was crucial to Lean succeeding. That's why we're going next week."

"Oh, I get it. This is another one of those customer requirements. Go Lean or don't keep our business," Tuck said, looking disgusted.

"No, Tuck, you don't get it. Aeroquip isn't forcing us. in fact, Paul's doing a favor for us by letting us attend next week, instead of having to wait for their suppliers' seminars that won't be for a couple of months."

"John, let me be honest. I don't want to see us waste time, since waste is on your mind right now. Since the company is in trouble, I think we should do what we've always done in the past. Why argue with success? Let's tighten our belts and light a fire under the sales department."

"You have a paradigm."

"A what?" Tuck said.

"A paradigm. You're holding fast to a set of beliefs and not willing to look at any other alternatives."

"Is that something else Paul told you?"

"As a matter of fact, no. Mike, the new kid, told me that. He said that Tri-Star was doing set-ups in under an hour and measuring in minutes."

"Christ, what does a new employee know about how we do business?" Tuck said.

"Not much but he seems to know a lot about how Tri-Star does business."

"What's a huge company like Tri-Star have in common with us?"

"Is that your mind I hear slamming shut?" John asked. He leaned back in his chair and folded his arms over his chest.

"No, but...but...aw, hell, John. I don't know. Maybe it is."

"I'm not saying we're going Lean. All I am saying is we are attending that seminar next week and we're both going in with open minds."

Tuck nodded and let out a sigh.

"Do you think this is going to be easy for me?" John asked.

"Sure. You're always looking a hundred miles down the road. You built this company with vision, sweat and damned good insights. I'd be a fool not to recognize that."

"Thanks, but I'm not the world's most open-minded person. Do you know how long it took me to start wearing my seat belt?"

"Uhhh, no."

"Three tickets."

Tuck smiled. He'd always respected John and especially his ability to look at his own weaknesses.

"Three tickets, huh?"

"Yes. But I wear a seatbelt now."

"A week-long seminar. It's been years since I was in school. I haven't sat for eight hours straight since I was eighteen. That seminar's going to kill me," Tuck said.

"Eight o'clock Monday morning at Aeroquip. I'll meet you there," John said.

After Tuck had left his office, John had to admit Tuck was right. He'd never been big on going to seminars. He'd always questioned what an outsider could teach him about his business. That was another paradigm he discovered in himself. His own stubbornness at not looking at new ideas. John pondered on the last forty-eight hours then began reflecting on all of the changes in his life; his divorce, buying out Doug, new business demands. He was snapped out of his musings by the ringing of his personal telephone line in his office.

"Good afternoon, John. It's Slater. The test results came back and that disc is slightly ruptured. It's going to require surgery," his doctor informed him.

"What's the alternative?" John asked.

"There really isn't any. You don't have to have the surgery immediately but the longer you wait, the worse it's going to get. It won't heal on its own."

"Do you think I can safely put it off for six months?"

"That'd be stretching it."

"This is not a good time for me to be having surgery," John said.

"Tell me, when is a good time for someone to stab you in the back?"

"Your bedside manner leaves a lot to be desired," John said. "Seriously, can you keep me on my feet for six months?"

"If you're very careful, probably. You're going to have to take it easy, spend a lot of time resting and stop doing anything the second you feel even a twinge in your back. Don't use the muscle relaxers I prescribed unless it's absolutely necessary. The pain will be the only indication of how quickly it's deteriorating."

"Okay."

"John, I'm serious. Take it easy and keep your stress to a minimum. Give me a call if you have problems."

His office began to feel claustrophobic to him and he needed fresh air. Instead of going out through the shop, he went out the front door and walked around to the back field. As he walked, his noticed tightness in his back and knew it was stress making things even worse.

He went to his favorite rock and sat down. He tried appreciating the rich amber and purple sky caused by the setting sun but it didn't work and he realized that he was hoping to see Jimmy and Profit.

"Mr. Macchia!" a woman's voice called out and John looked back toward the shop.

Jimmy, Profit and a woman were walking toward him.

"Hi, John," Jimmy said.

"You call him Mr. Macchia, Jimmy," the woman said.

"It's okay. I told him to call me John. You must be Jimmy's mother."

"Yes, I'm Joyce McAlvey." She was carrying a covered dish and handed it to John.

"Jimmy has told me how much you've helped him and I wanted to thank you. It's an apple pie. It's also a bit of a gamble. It's a new recipe I got from my sister and this is the first time I've tried it."

John removed the cover and the aroma of freshly baked apple pie drifted into the air.

"This isn't necessary," he said.

"I'm sure it's not but Jimmy said you were letting him play in your field and I wanted to thank you."

"Thank you for the pie. It's been a long time since I've had home-baked pie."

"Well, just tell Jimmy how it is. I really would like to know so I can either keep the new recipe or toss it out."

"Let's go, Jimmy," she said heading back toward their car.

Profit's ears perked up and he bolted into field.

"Mom, I can't leave now. I have to find him."

"Okay, just home before dark," she said and left.

"Come on, Jimmy," John said. "We'll both go find Profit."

8

Bright and early Monday morning, John and Tuck sat patiently waiting for the Lean manufacturing seminar to start at Aeroquip.

Tuck started squirming in his seat, saying "I can't believe we're going to be sitting in here for a week." Before John could answer, the seminar leader walked to the front table.

"Good morning, ladies and gentlemen of the Aeroquip Corporation. I'm Ben Taylor, the seminar leader. As you know, Sam Jones, our CEO, has committed Aeroquip to the Lean manufacturing process and that's what we're here to accomplish. Getting all of your plants up to speed on Lean. As you may not know, we're also rolling this seminar out to our suppliers in a couple of months. However, we have the pleasure of John Macchia and Randy Tucker of ATMI joining us this week. ATMI has been a valued supplier of Aeroquip for several years and we're looking forward to their feedback." He led a round of applause for John and Tuck.

"We're going to be spending a great deal of time this week looking at our St. Louis plant. Dick, please come up here," he said to Dick Kindleson, the plant manager of the St. Louis facility. "We did an assessment a couple of months ago which will be our roadmap for how to best institute Lean at St. Louis. Please note I said 'how to' institute, not 'think about', not 'consider', not 'contemplate', but 'how to' institute Lean at St. Louis. Sam Jones is absolutely, fully committed to Lean and so is every employee who has a future at Aeroquip."

As Ben clicked on the computer projector, he said, "Speaking is awfully dusty work," and paused to pour some water into a Styrofoam cup. He took a sip, set the cup back down and poured in more water. Still holding on to the pitcher of water, he began walking around the room.

"Have you ever thought of what a precious resource water is?" he asked the group. "Water is the staff of life. It is—" and was cut off by Dick Kindleson who said, "Your cup's leaking, Ben."

"It is?" Ben asked and quickly returned to the front of the room. "So it is. Would you pick it up and give me a hand here, Dick?"

Dick picked up the Styroform cup, making sure that the spouting water was away from him, not toward him.

"Boy, that's a mess," Ben said. "Here. It just needs more water," he said as he quickly poured water into the cup. Several more leaks appeared, creating a spray affect. Dick held the cup at arm's length and started to set the cup down when Ben said, "Oh, no, Dick. Don't set that cup down. Water's a precious resource. We need every drop of it." To everyone's surprise, he added more water to the over-brimming cup.

"Watch it!" Dick said, the water in the cup overran the brim, soaking his hand.

"We can't let this precious resource get away from us," Ben said, pouring more water into the cup. "We have to keep every drop."

"Then quit wasting it!" Dick said, moving away from Ben. He sat the cup down on the table and shook his drenched hand.

"Waste?" Ben said. "Were we wasting it?" he asked facetiously. "Thanks for being a good sport, Dick. Yes, ladies and gentlemen, we were wasting that water. Eliminating waste is what Lean is all about."

Tuck whispered to John, "He dumps water on me and there'll be a problem," but realized that John didn't hear him. John was transfixed.

Clicking the remote control to the computer that brought up the first slide, Ben said, "We're going to start by taking a look at the seven deadly wastes."

The slide read:

SEVEN DEADLY WASTES

OVER PRODUCTION
EXCESSIVE INVENTORY
TRANSPORTATION
WAITING
MOTION
OVER PROCESSING
CORRECTION OF DEFECTS

As Ben looked at the slide, he said, "I don't know about the rest of you but I've sat through a hundred seminars and just because some so-called expert said something, I didn't necessarily believe it was true. I'm from Missouri. Show me! Speaking of Missouri, we're going to take a long, hard look at the St. Louis plant."

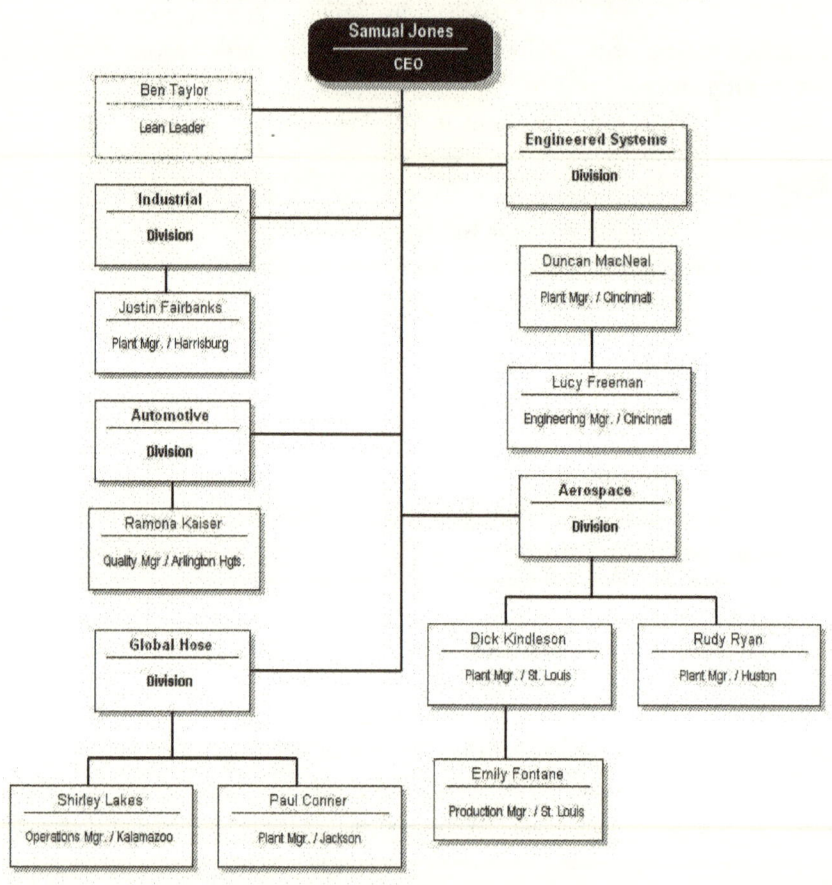

AEROQUIP Organization Chart

Key Employees Who Attended the Lean Seminar

He passed around a stack of training manuals, saying, "Everyone, please take one. Before we get started on St. Louis, I want to make it very clear that St. Louis is one of our very best plants and that's one of the reasons it was slated to convert to Lean later than some of the rest of the plants."

"If we're doing so well, why not leave us alone?" Dick asked, laughing but with a hint of seriousness in his voice.

"Because doing 'so well' isn't enough to keep Aeroquip competitive and it isn't world-class," Ben said. "Dick, I know you're from Missouri, too, and this can't be easy for you. My only advice is to depersonalize this as much as possible. This is not an attack on you, your people or your plant. We're using St. Louis as the working model for this seminar and what you'll find is that even a plant that's doing well, very well, in fact, can improve significantly by converting to Lean."

Once everyone had a manual, he said, "Please turn to page 14. What you see are the actual numbers for the St. Louis plant. For those of you who don't know, the St. Louis plant produces the cockpit panels for commercial airplanes. Now, let's take a look at the first deadly waste. Over production."

He went to the white board and wrote 'over production.' "Last year, St. Louis produced 412 cockpit panels against a purchase order calling for 375 cockpit panels. That's 37 more than the client ordered."

"There's a reason for that," Dick protested. "We always overproduce to make sure we have enough."

"Does your wife cook seven steaks if there are going to be six guests for dinner?" Ben asked.

"Not unless someone's really hungry," Dick said, laughing.

"Did you need the extra 37 cockpit panels?"

"As a matter of fact, we did need some of them."

"Because…?"

"Well, because…because a few didn't pass inspection so it was a good thing that we had so many as back-up. It kept the customer happy."

"Ummm…" Ben said. "Okay. However, if you'd produced 375 good cockpit panels that did pass inspection, would you have needed the extra 37?"

"What if they'd increased their order?" Dick asked. "We would've been ahead of the game."

"True, or so it seems. The question is, though, did they increase their order?"

"No."

"On to point two. Excessive inventory. To produce one cockpit panel for the 727, you need 14 different lenses. Correct? The lenses cover such mechanisms as the fuel gauge, the altimeter, auto-pilot, and so on, and the 727 requires 14 different, non-interchangeable lenses."

"Correct."

"According to the records from the St. Louis assessment, in your inventory for the 727, you have 101 lenses for altimeter, 46 lenses for the fuel gauge, and 38 for the auto-pilot. As of 45 days ago when the assessment was done, your inventory showed 589 extra lenses for the 727."

"I'll take your word for it," Dick said.

"589 lenses in inventory for the cockpit panel of a plane that is never going to be produced again."

"We had no way of knowing they were going to discontinue the 727," Dick protested.

"I'm not suggesting you did or that you ordered all of the extra lenses that are now in your inventory by mistake. You did it to make sure you had enough on hand to meet your customer's demand."

"That's right," Dick said, feeling somewhat vindicated.

"But now, that same decision has resulted in 589 lenses for a plane that's never going to be produced again."

Before Dick could answer, Ben continued, "St. Louis purchased the extra lenses and is paying for warehousing them with no hope of recouping those costs."

Dick was silent.

"Now, on to transportation. St. Louis spent $ 375,000 in expedited shipping costs. Dick, this isn't to attack but to explore. My guess is that your staff has the sense that the majority of that cost was due to unreasonable customer demands."

"Yes, and that's my sense, too."

"After careful analysis by the infamous bean counters, $ 50,000 was due to client changes. $50,000 which was billed and paid by the customer. The St. Louis accounting department is very accurate so congratulations on that. The $ 375,000 is in addition to the $ 50,000. Dick, these numbers are sobering. I can't stress enough that this is not an attack session. As I said earlier and will reiterate, St. Louis is one of Aeroquip's best plants. What was uncovered during the assessment is significantly fewer problems than at most plants."

"But still, they need to be corrected," Dick said.

"Yes," Ben said.

"And, without further waiting, let's take a look at waiting," Ben said. "In the St. Louis plant, on the line that produces the cockpit panel, the machine cycle time is 17 minutes." Ben went to the white board and said, "Let's do a bit of quick math," he said as he began writing on the board. "Seventeen minutes means three cycles per hour. Three multiplied by 17 is 51 minutes. It takes two minutes to load, and two minutes to unload each cycle which equals 12 minutes. And, let's assume that for 9 minutes, the operator is straightening up the area, doing routine maintenance and what-not. That means that for every hour, that operator is not working for thirty minutes. Dick, have you told your employees that you've given them a fifty-percent increase in their hourly wage?"

"I did no such thing," Dick protested.

"Not intentionally. One of the mistakes we've made for a long time is paying people by the hour, paying for their time, rather than their contribution. The fact is that Aeroquip is paying every operator on that line to stand around and do nothing for thirty minutes of each hour."

"There are things they are supposed to be doing!" Dick protested. "I don't allow my employees to just stand around."

"Don't personalize this, Dick. The most important job that operator has is to see to it that the machine keeps operating, right? That means that everything else comes second. The priority is getting parts in and out of that machine and I know your employees are some of the best. They're not intentionally taking advantage of the company. It's the way we set it up. Our employees are doing what we asked them to do."

Dick didn't respond.

John reflected on his encounter with the three ATMI employees, Carter, Hank and Roy, who were standing around, waiting, and it was ATMI's responsibility. He knew exactly what Ben was talking about.

"Now, ladies and gentlemen, I'd like to introduce you to Petey Part." He clicked the remote control device and the computer screen advanced, showing a small character that looked a lot like a spark plug, dancing on the screen. Petey Part was bright yellow, shiny and new, and beaming with a big smile.

"A few facts before we get started with the travels of Petey Part," Ben said. "The St Louis plant is 500,000 square feet. Petey Part comes into the plant off the south end receiving dock and is scheduled to leave four days later from the shipping dock on the southeast end of the building. How much traveling do you think Petey Part does in his four days at the St. Louis plant?"

He waited patiently for the group to answer. After a few moments, he said, "This seminar is not going to be all lecture. When I ask a question, if someone doesn't volunteer an answer, I'll pick someone," and he grinned.

Still no one answered.

"Okay. Emily, how far do you think Petey Part travels in his four days?"

Emily Fontane, Production Manager at St Louis, looked as though she'd just been struck with lightning, and took a deep breath before answering, "I'm not sure at all, but if the plant is 500,000 square feet, I'd guess he travels through the plant four times. I don't know how to convert that into linear feet."

"Good answer. Anyone else?"

When no one volunteered, Ben said, "Petey Part travels fifteen miles in four days."

"No way," Emily said.

"No one ever believes that when they first hear it, but it's true. "Let's watch," and he clicked the button on the computer that launched a short video clip. The background of the video showed the St. Louis plant and the foreground showed Petey Part's path through the plant with a bright red line. Petey Part started out bustling, bright, shiny and energetic. As the red line crisscrossed the plant again and again, Petey Part began sagging a bit. As the red line slashed across the plant repeatedly, Petey Part's path looked like a spider web made by a spider while on speed. When he was finished with his travels, Petey Part was at the shipping dock, looking downright haggard.

"Fifteen miles," Ben said, speaking softly as the video clip ended. "That's a lot of travel. You know, maybe we should be selling our parts as used, instead of new, given the mileage they have on them."

The audience laughed.

"Why does this part have to travel fifteen miles?" Ben asked.

The laughter stopped abruptly.

"You're all familiar with the three-trips-to-the-hardware-store-rule, aren't you? Any home improvement project will automatically require three separate trips to the hardware store. The first trip is for what you think you need. The second trip is for what you forgot. The third trip is for what you really need. Same principle is true here."

Dick spoke up. "I don't like where you're going with this at all, Ben. You're just a step away from suggesting we completely reorganize the plant. Do you have any idea of the cost involved in that?"

"As a matter of fact, I do. More importantly, I have a very good idea of the cost involved in not doing that."

As Dick started to speak again, Ben said as he held up his hands, "Don't tackle this one issue at a time. Let's wait until you see the full picture. Dick, you've been a great sport about all of this so far so keep up the good work," Ben said.

"Why does that sound like a warning?" Dick asked.

"Because the next question is a tough one. Do you know why your receiving department fills out Forms 4701-A and B?"

"Because it's part of the receiving process," Dick said. "I'm sure it helps us keep track of the raw material coming in."

"At one time, you would've been absolutely right. But that time was when St. Louis had two separate plants. Your plant purchased raw material in bulk which was the cheapest way to purchase it and a smart move. Your receiving department had to keep track of how much material went to Plant A and how much went to Plant B so Forms 4701-A and -B were created. But, when Plant B was shut down and this was before you got there, most of the machines were absorbed into Plant A while three machines were shipped to the Albuquerque facility. That action made Forms 4701-A and -B obsolete, especially since the receiving department also completes Material Assignment forms by product line. What's worse is that raw material can't be moved from the receiving dock until Forms 4701-A and -B are returned to them from the Production Department. During the assessment, raw material sat on the dock, waiting for those forms, and three machines went idle because they didn't have any raw material."

"I didn't know…" Dick said, his voice trailing off.

"We know. It's a great example of what happens when we always do things the way we've always done them. No one stops to ask why anymore and the result is a prime example of over processing."

Ben looked around the room, studying the participants.

"How many of you can think of things your facilities are doing and you don't know why? My guess is that everyone in this room has examples. Now, on to the last of the seven deadly wastes. At the St. Louis plant, you have 650 employees. Seventy-five are staff or salaried and 575 are hourly. Of the 575 hourly, 41 are inspectors. Your rework department also has four to seven employees in it per shift. If you're doing things right the first time, if accountability is with the person doing the work, your inspectors and rework employees are redundant because there would be no need for correction of defects."

Ben's last bombshell stunned the group into complete silence.

"Excuse me, Ben, but I'm the Quality Manager at the Arlington Heights facility and I can tell you we absolutely need our inspectors," Ramona Kaiser said. "You've made some very good points so far but there isn't any way we're going to eliminate our inspectors. So, we'll go along with this, use the good information that you're offering but there are some things that won't work at all of our facilities. Speaking strictly for Arlington Heights, we won't be getting rid of our inspectors." She folded her arms over her chest and leaned back in her chair. There were murmurs of assent from other participants.

"There are two ways I can answer that, Ramona," Ben said. "Let me use this approach first. Why do you need inspectors?"

"To make sure we're only sending quality parts to our customers," she said.

"So, we're in agreement that sending only quality parts to our customers is a major objective of Aeroquip."

"Yes," she said.

"Imagine for a moment that your operators knew when they were producing good or bad parts and did what was necessary to make sure only good parts were shipped. That would eliminate the need for the inspectors, right?"

"In an ideal world, maybe. But, people make mistakes. You can't expect an operator to know what's right or not. The Quality Department is there to make sure they're doing a good job, that nothing slips through the cracks."

"Why can't you expect an operator to know what's right or not?" Ben asked.

"Several reasons. They're not trained to understand all of the nuances of customer demand. Sometimes they're operating machines to fill in for absent employees and haven't had all the necessary training. I hate to say it, but some operators will get by with doing as little as possible. Our inspectors are our safety net that insures only quality parts get sent to the customer."

"So, let me ask this. If we made sure the operators did understand all of the nuances, if we provided sufficient cross training so employees were only operating machines they understood and if we got rid of those employees who were just doing enough to get by, would we still need inspectors?"

"Yes. Inspectors are the final authority and we need them."

"Aeroquip has eleven plants that are fully operational without inspectors. Their customer satisfaction ratings are the highest in the company."

"Be that as it may, Arlington needs its inspectors. You expect me to go back and fire all of our inspectors? What do you think that'll do to company morale?"

"Who said anything about firing them? In the rest of the plants, they've been redeployed where they could make greater contributions to the plant. Part of the Lean philosophy is that quality truly becomes a coaching process integration and not a police function."

"Maybe in your ideal world," Ramona said sarcastically.

"Now for the second approach," Ben said. "Ramona, you've brought up some interesting points. You say 'in my ideal world.' To everyone in this room, this seminar is your formal invitation to the ideal world I'm talking about. Of course, accepting the invitation is voluntary, but as Jack Welch said, 'You have the right not to change but not here.'"

"You're trying to tell me that this is a requirement?" Ramona asked.

"I'm not just trying. I am telling you that this is a requirement. Lean is a commitment that has been embraced by Aeroquip. Sam Jones is absolutely committed."

"It's just another tweak of the week," said Rudy Ryan, plant manager of the Houston plant.

"We've all been through 'tweaks of the week' before," Ben said. "However, Lean is not the latest fad. It's been around for a number of years. It was first utilized in the automotive industry in the United States to combat the Japanese onslaught. Now, other industries are playing catch-up with automotive. Aeroquip has 31 plants. Eleven have completely made the conversion to Lean. Twelve plants are in the conversion process. This group represents the last eight plants to be converted."

"You will be assimilated. Resistance is futile," Rudy said in his best Borg voice.

"You got it, Rudy. That's a very good analogy." Ben glanced at his watch. "No doubt it's tough sitting here so let's take a fifteen minute break but before we do, I'd like to give this to Dick." He reached under the podium and withdrew a jacket. He motioned for Dick to join him in the front of the classroom. After helping Dick put the jacket on, he asked Dick to turn around so everyone could see the bull's eye target on the back.

9

During the break, Paul walked up to John and Tuck and said, "What do you think so far?"

"I'm learning a lot," John said, taking a sip of coffee.

"Yeah, it's interesting," Tuck said, "But, it's not the kind of thing ATMI can do. I'm sure it's working for Aeroquip, but it won't work for us."

"Why do you say that, Tuck?" Paul asked.

Before he could answer, Ramona nudged her way into their group and tapped Paul on the arm.

"Paul, I've known you for twenty years. What is all of this crap? Get rid of the inspectors? I don't think so."

"Ramona, we haven't had inspectors in six months."

"That might work here in Jackson, but it will not work in Arlington Heights. I can tell you that right now, no matter what this Ben Taylor says."

"He's here with the complete backing of Sam Jones. Don't forget that. I think you've locked into a paradigm and can't see any other way."

"Look, he said they were waiting to convert the best plants. If Arlington's one of the best plants, which it is, why mess with it?"

"The other plants that were converted first were not doing as well as Arlington Heights or the rest of the plants represented here. In fact, a couple of them were hemorrhaging. That's all been reversed. I know it seems impossible to even think of working without inspectors but we'll take a tour of our facility here and you can see it in operation."

"Here is not Arlington Heights," she said pointedly. "It won't work in Arlington Heights."

"Wasn't that just what you were saying, Tuck?" John asked.

Tuck could see that Ramona had blinders on and wasn't willing to listen to any new ideas. He didn't want to put himself in that camp.

"I just said we're a job shop and it might be different for us," Tuck said.

"That's one of the neat things about Lean," Paul said. "The principles are the same but allow a great deal of flexibility. It's like exercising. We all know it's good for us but there isn't just one exercise, like jogging, that's best. The key is to understand the principles and apply them in the way that will do the most good for your company."

"I can't believe what he did to Dick, either. Humiliating him like that. The poor man," Ramona said.

"Humiliating him? Is that what you saw?" John asked.

"Yes. Didn't you?"

"No. I saw Ben review the facts of what was happening at Dick's plant and didn't hear him attack Dick at all. I can see where it might've been hard for Dick, but they both handled it well. We need that kind of assessment done at ATMI," John said.

"We do?" Tuck asked, clearly surprised.

"Yes. An assessment seems like just the tool for us to help us see where we need the most help now."

Ben walked up to the group and clapped John on the back.

"John, thanks so much for coming. I hate to use the term 'guinea pig,' but you're our first supplier to attend our seminars and I'm really eager to hear your feedback."

"So far, it's been very informative. I was just saying I want to do a Lean assessment at ATMI like you did in St. Louis."

"I'll get an assessment form for you. Right now," he glanced around the small group, "Let's head back and get started again."

Once the group had settled back into their seats, Ben began, "Dick, let's talk about the parts that St. Louis produces. What are St. Louis' core competencies? Simply put, core competencies are what your plant does well."

"We produce the interior dash for cockpits and we do it extremely well," Dick said with pride.

"Yes. You have a great reputation with our customers. Now, let's talk about the nickel-plating done in St. Louis."

"Do we have to?" Dick said in mock horror.

"Yes, we do. St. Louis nickel plates one control lever that goes on the interior wall of the cockpit, right?"

"Yes."

"Since St. Louis has devoted a significant amount of capital resources to this product, plating's not cheap as we all know, as well as labor, it must be a real cash cow for you."

"Ben, that's just mean of you," Dick said, smiling. "You know that we lose money on every lever we produce. It'd be cheaper if we just sent a ten-dollar bill to the customer for every lever they wanted."

"Now I'm confused. You've made a huge capital investment in the process but you lose money on every part. Hmmm...Why do you keep producing it?"

"It was a bundled product. If we wanted the dashboards, we had to agree to the lever. And, there wasn't any way the customer would pay us enough to make money on the lever. We bit the bullet to keep the customer happy."

"To state the obvious, then, if you weren't producing the lever, your plant would be far more profitable, correct?"

"Not only in terms of hard profit, but in terms of less stress, less grief, absolutely. I hate that part!" Dick said, slapping his palm on the table top for emphasis.

"Okay. That's quite understandable." To the group, he said, "I'm sure everyone sees Dick's dilemma. What are some options?"

He went to the white board and waited for their responses. As people called out ideas, he wrote them down and ended up with a list.

Raise the prices on the lever
Refuse the dashboard business
Increase the plating business
Sub-contract the lever to another company
Convince the customer to not use a nickel-plated lever

"Good ideas," Ben said to the group. "How is it that we've allowed this to happen to us? And, aren't we also doing it to our suppliers? Asking them to do things that are not in their core competencies." He looked at John. "John, has Aeroquip ever asked you to produce a part...let me rephrase that. Has Aeroquip ever required you to produce a part that wasn't a core competency for you? Please speak freely."

Tuck burst out in laughter.

"Tuck, what's up?" Ben asked. "I take it Aeroquip has done that."

Still laughing, Tuck said, "Ohhh, well, sure, but what I'm laughing about was your telling John to speak freely. He doesn't know how to do anything else!"

"Really?" Ben asked.

"Oh, yeah. In fact, ask him about the rubberized nozzle Aeroquip required us to do. We were in production for just a year, thank God. I don't know which would've worn out first, the machine or John's foot." By this time, Tuck was laughing so hard, tears were steaming down his face.

"Hells bells," John said. "I'm not a rubberizer or vulcanizer. I'm a machinist. That's what ATMI does and better than anybody else. Aeroquip insisted that they wanted that…that rubberized nozzle shipped with the Part 4445 so we did it."

"How much did it cost you?" Ben asked.

"More than I'm going to admit in public," John answered. "But, I know what Dick meant about shipping a ten dollar bill with each part."

"Folks, we're just talking common sense here. Why would we do this to our valued suppliers? Why would we let our customers do it to us? Would you ask your dentist to set a broken arm? Of course not, but we've been doing exactly that for years. Every time a company steps out of its' core competencies, it's a disaster."

Rudy spoke up, saying "I don't know about that. We've developed a very profitable line because a customer called and asked for something we didn't normally do. Our engineers grabbed a hold of it and we're doing it. It's a nice little profit center for Houston. I'm not going to be turning away any chance for profit."

"Are you at full capacity with this new product or are you selling the same type of product to other customers?" Ben asked.

"We're selling to four customers now so it's been good growth for us. We're at about 80% capacity."

"What you did, without knowing it, was make that new product one of your core competencies. You've proven my point, Rudy. Thank you," Ben said.

"Glad it worked out that way for you," John said, "But as Tuck mentioned, it didn't work out that way for us. We're top-notch machinists. He wasn't joking about my kicking the machine. I see what Ben's saying. Now, let me ask you, Ben. When Aeroquip asks for a product that isn't…isn't a core competency, I'm free to tell them 'No'?"

"Saying 'No' is always your right, John. But, let's not be black and white about this. Consider sub-contracting a part that's not in your core competencies or if the demand is going to be high enough, increasing your core competencies to include it before you just say 'No.' If those two options don't work, the Lean philosophy is that you decline the order."

"How's Aeroquip going to react to that?" John asked.

"That is an excellent question," Ben answered. "Paul, how do you respond to that?"

"In the good, old days, we'd not be concerned about our suppliers' core competencies. We'd just tell them what we want and expect it. With the Lean philosophy of working with suppliers, it's different but still…"

"If they want our business, they better do it," Rudy broke in. "It's what we do for our customers. Same thing applies to our suppliers."

"Used to apply," Ben said. "Step back from it. What's the goal you want to accomplish?"

"Profit," Rudy answered without hesitation.

"We'd all agree that our suppliers help to make us profitable, right?" Ben asked. "So, why ask them to do something that's not a core competency?"

John thought of the beagle pup, chasing helplessly after a Frisbee he couldn't possibly catch.

"Woof," John said, causing everyone to look at him.

"Woof?" Ben asked, his eyebrows raised.

"Woof. This is a lesson I taught a young boy about his beagle puppy just last week. Paul, here's the answer. If you ask ATMI to do a part that's not in our core competency, here's what we're going to do. If it's an emergency, we'll do everything we can to help you out. Always know that. But, other than an emergency, we're going to attempt to sub-contract it with a reliable company or we're going to determine whether the part can become a core competency. Barring that, we're going to turn down the business."

Tuck choked on his coffee, sputtering, "We are?"

"Yes, we are. I'm done kicking machines," John said. "Paul, my goal is to do the very best work I can for you. It's not our best work if I'm kicking machines, my employees are fumbling around with no expertise, and I'm lighting a match to dollar bills. It's not good for you and it's not good for us. I hope you're comfortable with that."

Ben grinned knowingly. "Yes, John, on behalf of Aeroquip, we're comfortable with that. Aren't we, Paul?"

"You mean I'm not going to get to beat up our suppliers anymore?" Paul asked asked mischievously.

"That's horse manure," Rudy flatly stated. "Our suppliers are there to serve us. They hadn't better be telling me 'No,' or they can kiss the Aeroquip business good-bye."

A chill fell over the room.

"Whatever our suppliers do for us, it has to meet our quality standards," Ramona said, adding her two cents' worth. "If they take the business, I expect it to be perfect."

"How do you help them achieve that?" Ben asked Ramona.

"Help them? That's not the way it works. They're here to help us," she answered.

"Aeroquip is developing partnership relationships with our suppliers," Ben said. "That's the Lean philosophy. I can see we need to do some attitude adjustment here."

"I'm not adjusting my attitude," Rudy said defiantly. "I'm the customer. Pure and simple. My suppliers better do what I ask or it's bye-bye supplier."

Seeing the battle lines being quickly drawn, John spoke up.

"I'm a supplier to Aeroquip and have been for a number of years. We blew a shipment last week and when I went to Aeroquip, I expected to get my ears pinned back by Quality, Engineering, Production, Sales and the janitorial staff. That's what had always happened in the past. What happened is that Paul invited us to this seminar and has offered to help us look at our processes to make improvements. It's one thing to hire our machines and our labor. It's another to win our hearts. On behalf of ATMI, I can tell you that we'll bend over backwards to be the best supplier they've ever had."

"Who gives a damn about your hearts?" Rudy asked.

"I do," Paul said.

"So does Aeroquip as a company," Ben said. "Remember, Lean is not only a manufacturing approach, it's more importantly a philosophy." Glancing at his watch, he said, "Let's break for lunch."

10

Ben walked down from the front of the room and approached John and Randy Tucker. "How would you two like to join me and Paul for lunch?

Tuck looked at John. "I was planning on going back to the shop John, just to make sure everything is running smoothly. Why don't you go on? I'll just grab something to eat on the way back."

John said, "Ok, Tuck, but, remember to make it back here on time for the afternoon session. I don't want you to get tied up with some project back at the shop."

"No problem, I'll be back by 1:00 p.m. sharp." Tuck shook Ben's hand, thanked him for the morning session and left the room.

John shook his head. "That guy practically lives at the shop. Nothing goes on without his knowing about it. I guess that's why I like him so much. As long as he's around, I know things get done the way they're supposed to."

"What happens when he's not around," Ben asked?

John paused a second, cocked his head, shrugged and said, "You know I can't ever remember him not being around. He never gets sick, won't take a vacation and when he's not around, he's calling in every hour to check up on us."

Ben looked over at Paul and motioned for him to join them. As the three of them walked out to the car, Ben said, "John, I get the sense that both you and Tuck are hands-on managers. You both like to be in the thick of things. You like to solve problems and most of your employees come to you for answers when things get tough. Would that be a fair observation?"

John nodded toward Paul and good naturedly said, "With guys like this around, I better have the answers. If I don't, I'll be out of business."

"I understand that," Ben said. "However, if you adopt a Lean system, you're going to have to share the knowledge. It has to become a team effort."

As they reached the car, Paul leaned down and unlocked the door. The three men got in as Paul slid into the driver's seat.

"What are you guys in the mood for?" Paul asked.

"Something light and quick," responded John. Ben nodded.

"How about Gilbert's? They have a great buffet and you can have as little or as much as you want to eat and it's close," said Paul.

The other two men agreed and Paul put the car into gear and moved out of the parking lot.

As the car moved toward the expressway, John looked over at Ben and said, "You mentioned teamwork. That's not going to be a problem with us. I have some the best and most dedicated employees in the industry working for me. I never lose sight of the fact that their effort and contribution is what's made us a success. We are a team already." John spoke with the conviction of a man who deeply believed in what he was saying.

"I can attest to that, Ben," said Paul. "It's one of the reasons that ATMI is one of our best suppliers."

"I know that," said Ben. "That's why we were so interested in having you attend this seminar. Your reputation for integrity, hard work and customer service is above reproach. Just the type of company we want as an example of what Lean Manufacturing can do for our suppliers. If anybody can make it work, I know you can. By the same token, it's important to understand that there's a difference between team spirit and teamwork. It's more about a process than about an attitude. As part of that process, it may require you to help your team members get the answers for themselves rather than having them come to you and Tuck for them. That way, both you and Tuck can take a vacation without worrying about whether things are done right or not."

"Above all else, John," said Paul. "It all starts with you and your commitment to making it work. Don't adopt a Lean philosophy because you think Aeroquip wants you to. It has to make sense to you. You have to believe it's going to make you a better company. You'll have to develop a passion for it. Then, you'll have to ignite a passion in all your employees."

As they arrived at the restaurant, parked the car and were shown to their table, John kept thinking about Paul's words, *'You'll have to ignite a passion in all your employees.'*

They went through Gilbert's famous buffet line. One line for each possible entrée, salads, meats, vegetables, deserts, breads and drinks. The choices were endless. John was an example of restraint as he made himself a salad with lite Italian dressing and measured out a cup of onion soup without the melted cheese he loved so much.

After they sat back down, John said, "I told you I had some of the best employees in the industry working for me. And, while that's true, they're also pretty independent. Some might even say stubborn. I'm not sure I would be able to get them to accept some of the changes you're talking about, much less get them to develop a passion for them. And, from what I saw in this morning's session, you've got a couple of those independent types working for you, too."

"You mean Ramona and Rudy?" said Ben, more as a statement than a question.

"Yes," said John. "I've got a couple Rudy's and Ramona's back at the shop. If I try to force this on them, I'd probably lose them. It's also going to be a bit of a task to get Tuck on board, too."

"John, I think it's important to understand you probably are going to lose some people if you decide to make the changes we're taking about. However, while nobody likes to lose people, it may not be as bad as you think," Paul said. "If you've got people who are unwilling to change to improve your business, you may be better off without them. Plus, with the improvements you make with these changes, you'll eliminate enough man hours so you won't have to replace them."

"We're going to make every effort to get the Rudy's and Ramona's that work for us to change," said Ben. "But, we know full well that, with some, we'll fail. It all has to do with why people resist change. Why do you think people resist change?"

John thought for a moment. "I think there are a lot of reasons. I know that my brother resisted using computers for the longest time because he was scared to death of them. He convinced himself that they were too complicated and he would never be able to learn how to use the programs. That was until his kids showed him how. Now he doesn't go anywhere without his notebook or hand-held computer."

"Exactly! That's one of the biggest reasons people resist change. They don't believe they have the knowledge or skill needed to make the change," Ben said. "In that case, you have to provide those people with the training and education that will help them succeed. And, you have to do it in a way that doesn't make them feel stupid."

"Remember, John," Paul continued. "Resistance to change is about loss. When people are required to change, they're likely going to have to give up something. In this case, they're giving up the security and confidence of knowing what to do. They feel vulnerable and at a loss of what to do next. As they become trained and more comfortable in a new way of doing things in the new system, their resistance is dramatically reduced. In fact, if the new system helps them perform better and eliminates stress, the resistance is not only reduced, they will exhibit that passion for change that we talked about."

"That's right," said Ben. "People will change for two reasons. They're either presented with a short term threat or some long term benefit. The primary reason that Lean manufacturing took a hold in this country was due to the threat of off-shore competition in the automotive industry. It was a matter of survival. But, once in place, companies saw the long-term benefit of increased production, improved quality, better customer relations and finally increased profitability.

As Ben spoke, John couldn't help but think back to what Joel had warned him about the business, only a couple days ago. He understood all about short-term threats. That was the primary reason he was at the seminar. Not realizing he was thinking out loud, John mumbled to himself, "It can be a strong motivator, all right."

"What's that, John?" asked Paul

"Oh, nothing," responded John. Changing the subject, John said, "So, are you telling me I'm going to have to threaten my employees to get them to change?"

"Not at all," said Paul. "For most of our people, we emphasized the long term benefits that Lean would bring. That was enough to bring them on board. Once they saw how easily the system improved their performance and reduced their stress levels, they were sold."

"Even people like Rudy and Ramona?" John asked.

Paul sat back in his chair and took a bite of the blackened Sea Bass he had gotten from the buffet. John waited for a response.

"No, Rudy, Ramona and people like them are a different story," said Paul, as he wiped his mouth with a napkin and took a sip of coffee. "You want to explain, Ben?" asked Paul.

"Sure," said Ben. "We've talked about people resisting change because they were afraid to learn a new skills and knowledge. There are other reasons, too. Some people resist change because they fear the loss of their organizational position and power. Take Ramona, for example," Ben continued. "There's a strong probability that when the Lean systems are implemented in Arlington Heights, her department will drastically be cut, if not eliminated. Most certainly her power in the organization will be affected. She's no dummy. She can see the handwriting on the wall."

"Going back to what you said before, she'll experience a real loss, her job," observed John.

"Yes," said Ben. "Oh she wouldn't be fired. She'd be re-deployed in another area. But it's a loss just the same. You have to empathize with her feelings. That's one of the reasons I've cut her some extra slack in the seminar. The only other thing you can do is emphasize the positive long-term benefits for her, and hope that's enough."

"What about Rudy?" asked John. "Where does he fit in?"

"I can answer that," said Paul. "I've been in his position. Let's be honest," Paul continued. "Aeroquip is a large political company. Plant managers have always been rewarded for getting results. I've always thought our company mantra should have been, 'JUST DO IT', not Nike's. Rudy comes from a successful plant whose success has been largely due to his leadership. Now, to have someone from outside the plant come in and say we're going to do everything different…that's a hard pill to swallow."

"So, in other words, 'If I didn't invent I, I don't want to do it.' Is that what you're saying?" asked John.

"Well, that may be a bit harsh, John, but yes, that's basically what I'm saying," said Paul.

"What do you do about that?" inquired John.

"The only thing you can do is make him feel as though he's part of the process," said Ben. Get him involved in the decision making."

John smiled, and said "Make him think it's his idea."

Paul laughed out loud. "John, that's what I like about you. You know how to cut to the quick of the matter. But, yes, in a matter of speaking, that's exactly what has to be done. Fortunately, there's a lot of opportunity for that in the Lean process, if Rudy can work as part of a team."

"What if he can't?" John countered.

"Before I answer that question, is anybody going to tackle the desert line?" asked Ben. Both John and Paul indicated they were full. Ben looked at his waistline and decided that he wasn't brave enough to venture there alone. He needed a co-conspirator and since none was available, he sat back in his chair and motioned to the waitress to bring the check.

"John, you'll find that people will give you one of four levels of support for change," Ben began. "The first level are those that will help make it happen. They'll be vital to your success and must include your key people. The next group of people will be those who will let it happen. Once they see it working, they will get the passion. The next two levels are the most difficult. There will be those that moderately oppose the changes and there will be those that actively oppose them. The old 80/20 rule usually applies here. 80% of your people will fall into the first two groups and 20% will fall into the last two groups. Of the 20% that oppose the changes, 80% can be converted to the positive side. Unfortunately, 20% of those that oppose the changes will never support it. They will either decide to leave or will have to be asked to leave. That's the long and short of it."

John just nodded with a knowing smile.

"There is one other thing that you should be aware of," said Paul. "If you decide to implement Lean systems at ATMI, there is going to be a certain amount of stress for all your people as you implement it. Be on the lookout for people who might have other additional stress in their lives. These are people who may have personal problems at home or other stressors unrelated to work. You may want to ease up on them a bit when you define expectations. I know you've worked with Bob Dennison, our production manager."

"Oh, yes, I like Bob a lot," said John.

"When we started implementing the Lean systems at our plant, Bob was recovering from the death of his wife," said Paul. "He had the added pressure of learning how to be both mother and father to his four kids while dealing with his own grief. We wanted to implement quickly so our expectation on everybody were high. Long days and weekends were commonplace. I noticed that a number of things that had been assigned to Bob just weren't getting done. After talking to him, I realized that he just couldn't handle the workload with everything else that was going on in his life. I didn't want to lose him so I backed off on my expectation of him. I reassigned some things and took the pressure off him. I think he was grateful and has been one of our biggest supporters ever since."

John thought for a moment about his own life. He had more than a little stress himself to deal with. Unfortunately, he didn't have the luxury of reducing the expectations he had of himself. But, he would remember the lesson if he decided to embrace the Lean process for ATMI.

"You've given me a lot to think about. Both this morning and here at lunch," said John. "I appreciate your time. Thank you."

"No, we appreciate your time, John," said Paul. Ben nodded in agreement.

The drive back to the seminar was quiet as John sorted through all he had taken in during the last five hours.

11

After getting the group settled down after lunch, Ben asked everyone to divide into two teams and go to separate sides of the training room.

"We're going to do an experiment," he said, after the two groups got situated. "Everyone has a different perspective on Lean when they're first introduced to it so we're going to see if we can put some of the principles into practice and make a comparison."

He fired up the computer and the first slide read:

BENEFITS OF LEAN

Improved quality
Increased productivity
Enhanced customer satisfaction
Reduced operating costs

"Would everyone agree that these are benefits worth achieving?" he asked.

"Oh, sure," Rudy piped up, "What idiot is going to say they're not?"

"Rudy, I like that you speak your mind," Ben said. "You're right. No one is going to disagree with the potential benefits but what most people don't realize is the amount of the benefits that can be achieved." He clicked the remote control device and the next slide popped up.

BENEFITS OF LEAN

Improved quality—
Reduced defects by 20% per year
Improved quality by 85%
Increased productivity—
Increased typically by 35%
Enhanced customer satisfaction—
Reduced lead time by 70%
Increased on-time delivery to nearly 100%

Reduced operating costs—
Reduced inventory typically by <u>75%</u>

"I'll eat my hat if you can get those kinds of returns in Houston," Rudy said.

"Would you like that with Salsa," Paul asked. "I know the numbers are startling but we did even better."

"Must've had a lot of room for improvement then," Rudy retorted.

"Ouch," Ben said. "We're not going to let our conversations disintegrate into attacks."

"Thanks, Ben," Paul said, "But that's okay. He's right. Our plant needed a lot of help and as you said this morning, the best plants were kept until the last. He has a lot to be proud of in Houston."

"Damn straight," Rudy said. "No offense intended."

"All of the plants represented here today, except for Paul's, operate in a linear fashion right now. Lean emphasizes the one-piece-flow manufacturing process or cell manufacturing. They're really the same thing. With linear, an operator is responsible for doing part of the job, one element of the whole. The operator will do a single job repeatedly throughout the shift. We know that the operator should be checking for quality of the parts coming into his or her work area but the reality is they normally just accept what they're sent, do their part, and move them on down the line. Agreed?"

Most of the participants nodded in agreement.

"With Lean, an operator or a group of operators form a cell, and they're completely responsible for the quality of their parts. They make the entire product. So, the manufacturing floor that now has long production lines will look like a beehive with several cells. The operators have the right to reject the raw material coming into their cell, as well as scrapping parts they've produced. They don't depend on quality to tell them whether it's acceptable or not. Quality becomes a process function, and not a policing function. Once they're done, the parts are shipped to the customer."

"You seriously expect operators to know quality?" Ramona asked, her contempt barely concealed.

"Yes. It's been our experience that properly trained operators know a quality part better than the inspectors do. Operators are able to sense impending problems faster than anyone else in the plant. Therefore, problems are recognized earlier and fixed faster. More importantly, they're held accountable and responsible for their quality. Most importantly, Lean puts decision-making at the most effective level, the operator."

"That's nonsense," Ramona said.

"Let me make a comment," John said. "We have inspectors, too, and they're normally more in the loop about what our customers want, as well as knowing about changes, the acute or non-acute needs of the customer, than our machinists. However, our machinists know when a drill bit is going bad before it happens. They know when an alignment has shifted. They're the hands-on experts and I rely on their judgments. What Ben is saying is making sense to me. If we improved the communication with our machinists, or operators as in your case, they'd be able to do exactly what Ben is talking about."

"How many employees do you have?" Ramona asked.

"We have forty hourly employees," John answered.

"Of course it'd be easy under those circumstances, but Arlington Heights is a large plant. We have 700 operators. It's impossible…"

Ben's laughter interrupted Ramona and she stopped speaking mid-sentence.

"I'm sorry for laughing but the argument is normally that Lean can only work in the big plants and isn't suitable for the small or medium-sized manufacturers or job shops. It's humorous to see it being argued the other way."

"I don't find our quality operation being destroyed humorous in the least," Ramona said, obviously piqued.

"On the contrary," Ben said. Pointing to the slide, he continued, "We're talking about improving quality by 85% and reducing defects by 20% or more per year. Does it require a significant change in people, their attitudes, performance, training and management? Absolutely. Is it worth it? Absolutely."

"In your opinion," Ramona said.

"Not only in my opinion…" He paused. "Wait a minute. Ramona, are you saying that if Lean can do everything I'm saying it can, it wouldn't be worth it?"

"I'm saying that I don't have the confidence in this new system that you do," she answered.

"New? Lean has been around for a long time. It's well withstood the test of time. It's one of the key elements that kept U.S. automotive from failing completely under the Japanese onslaught. Twenty years ago, U.S. automotive was trailing behind every other U.S. manufacturing operation, except maybe coal mining. Right now, the most innovative, progressive and competent manufacturing in the United States is done in automotive. They're truly on the leading edge."

Ramona stayed silent, her lips pursed.

"Okay, on to our exercise. Both teams are going to be making paper airplanes. This is a timed exercise and each plane completed has to meet the established quality criteria to be accepted." Bending down, he retrieved two large boxes from beneath the speaker's podium. "Here are all of the supplies you'll need, including the quality standards. Team One, you're going to be using only Lean techniques and Team Two, you're going to be using only linear techniques."

He gave each team their box.

"Since Paul is familiar with Lean techniques, he is the team leader for Team One by default. Team Two, you get to choose your own leader."

John, as a member of Team One, sat down and waited for Paul to get everyone organized.

Tuck was on Team Two and immediately volunteered to be the Team Leader.

"Now, son," Rudy said, "We can all see how you'd like to be the leader of a team to compete against your boss and win. We'd all like to win so maybe we should take a long look at the experience in our group before rushing to a decision."

"*Son?*" Tuck thought and said, "That must be a Texas thing but whatever," and said no more.

"I think Rudy should be our team leader," Ramona said. "He's the plant manager of a big plant and knows about organizational success. I also think I should obviously be head of quality. We want the best people in each position, don't we?"

Tuck's jaw muscles tensed and untensed but he smiled and said, "Sure. Whatever works."

"If there are no further interruptions, let's get started," Rudy said. He looked at the specifications sheet for the paper airplanes. "Okay, we're going to need five stages in the production line since there are four parts to the airplane, fuselage, right wing, left wing, and tail, plus assembly. Ramona, can you handle quality all by yourself or will you need some help?"

"I can handle it all," she said.

"Great. Let's get started. Assembly shouldn't be hard so we'll have three lines funneling into assembly. Okay," he said, pointing to the first three people, "You're fuselage assembly and the start." Pointing to the next three people, he said, "You're right wing." Pointing to the next three people, he said, "You're left wing." Pointing to the next three people, he said, "You're tail," and pointed to the last person, saying, "You're final assembly." He divided the stack of paper into three roughly equal piles and handed it to the fuselage assembly people. "Get started."

Tuck found himself as a left-wing cutter with nothing to do but wait until the fuselage group got the hang of things.

Meanwhile, Paul gathered his group around and said, "We all need to learn quickly how to make paper airplanes. Does anyone have any experience?"

John said, "Not with paper, but I want to become a licensed pilot if that helps any and know a little about aviation. ATMI produces parts for aviation."

"If these specifications are true to life, you could help people understand the importance of the requirements," Paul said.

John looked at the spec. sheet and said, "I'm not sure about how realistic they are, but I'll help any way that I can."

Paul passed out twenty sheets of paper to each participant, then, he handed each one a sheet of green paper, a sheet of yellow paper and a sheet of red paper. "We're going to learn a quick kan-ban system first. Count out ten sheets of paper and put in the yellow sheet, then, count out seven more sheets and put in the red sheet of paper. Put the green sheet on top. When you start working, put the green sheet where it's visible to you and to me. A kan-ban is a simple inventory pull system that lets you and me know when you're running low on vital material. When I see the yellow sheet, I know your supplies are getting low and will replenish. If I see a red sheet at one person's work area and a yellow sheet at another, the red sheet will take precedence. That also means that I've made a mistake in not getting to the 'red sheet' person sooner when the yellow sheet was showing. What questions does anyone have on this?"

When no one asked anything, Paul passed out scissors with rounded tips, glue sticks, instruction sheets and patterns to each person.

"These are what I let my grandkids use," said Shirley Lakes, Operations Manager at the Kalamazoo plant, laughing out loud as she held up the rounded tip scissors.

"We're not supposed to run with them, either," Paul said, smiling.

"Don't tell me we have to worry about OSHA here, too?" Duncan MacNeil, plant manager from Cincinnati, asked. "Who's going to be making what parts?"

"Each person will be making a complete airplane," Paul answered. "It's cell manufacturing, or the focus factory. It's a key concept in Lean."

"Isn't that redundant?" Duncan asked. "Why should we all learn how to do everything? Isn't that going to take us longer and we'll lose?"

"It'll take us longer in the planning stages, right now," Paul said, glancing over at the other team where some members had already started cutting while others sat doing nothing. "But, we'll be faster in actual quality production. The key word is quality. You're going to be your own inspector. If you know you've cut a part wrong, throw it away. Don't save it. Don't event think about a rework department because they don't exist at Team One Airplane Manufacturing. Scrap the part and move on."

"Okay, bossman," Duncan said, saluting.

"Whoa. I'm not the boss," Paul said. "We're all team members with equal footing. Ben selected me because I have more experience with Lean or at least he thought I did. My job is to see that we complete this exercise using Lean principles, such as the kan-bans. All right. Let's get started. I'd like to suggest that we each make a plane and see how we do, who needs help, who's good at it, that sort of thing."

Without further discussion, Team One members began reading the instructions, and cutting the pattern pieces out for a complete plane.

Shirley was done first and said, "Now what?"

"Make your plane," Paul said. "Notice I said 'your' plane. Each person is responsible for his or her own mini-factory. We can get help from each other but we're each accountable for our own productivity and quality. Write your initials on an inside piece that won't show…"

"I see," Shirley said, "Then, you'll know who to blame."

"I'll know who to hold accountable and who to praise, too," Paul said. "Now, let's get started, shall we?"

Over on the other side of the room, Team Two was busily producing pieces according to the standard assembly-line approach. Stacks of wings, both right and left, were fast building up, as were fuselages and tails. Shortly, Justin Fairbanks, plant manager from Harrisburg, who was the assembly person, started the assembly process only to stop abruptly.

"I can't do this," he said to Rudy. "I'm allergic to Fast-stick glue. Sorry." He pushed away from the table as if he'd spotted a rattlesnake.

"Allergic?" Rudy asked.

"Yes, I'm allergic to all glues," Justin said.

"Why in hell didn't you tell me?" Rudy demanded.

"You didn't ask me. You just assumed I could do this job. Well, I can't," Justin said. "I can cut pieces but I can't touch the glue."

"Nothing like closing the barn door after the horses have run out," Rudy said. "Okay, switch places with…with her," he said, pointing to a woman who was cutting right wings.

"Lucy," said the woman. "My name is Lucy Freeman. I'm the Engineering Manager at Cincinnati. I work with Duncan MacNeil, the plant manager. Don't you think it'd be a good idea to find out if I'm allergic to the glue?" she asked.

Rudy glared at her.

"I'm not so you don't have to worry about it," she said. "Furthermore, I'm very good with crafts and should've been in this slot from the beginning."

"Okay, okay, so I blew it. Now can we get back to production?" Rudy said.

Lucy smiled sweetly and said, "Certainly. It'd be my pleasure. Besides, I'd like to see our team beat Duncan's."

Lucy and Justin switched places and production began again.

Lucy rapidly caught on to the assembly procedure and had glued three planes together when Ramona stopped by.

"The edges look out of alignment to me," Ramona said.

Lucy measured them and said, "They're within specifications."

"That may be but I think they'd look nicer with a closer alignment."

"You want me to redo the three I've already done?" Lucy asked.

"No. I'll let those go but on the rest of them, position the wings like this," Ramona said, showing Lucy what she expected.

The spirit of competition was high among the two teams as they raced against each other to complete as many planes as possible. Ben watched each group, carefully making notes. Team Two seemed very confident as each person passed on the cut parts to Lucy for assembly.

It was until she threw up her hands and said, "Time out, guys. This isn't working. I'm getting buried in plane parts and six people at the end aren't doing anything. I need some help down here."

"We aren't doing anything because we're already done," Tuck said. "We've completed our assignments. We did our jobs."

"Our job is to beat Team One," Lucy said, "And I need help now."

"There's another problem, too," Ramona said. "We have an excess of right wings and not enough left wings. Who blew it?"

"Time's up," Ben said.

Ben carefully checked the planes from Team One. Twenty-five planes passed inspection with none being rejected. He wrote the score on the white board. He then checked the planes from Team Two. Eighteen planes had been completed but only fifteen passed inspection, in spite of Ramona's protests that her change in alignment was an improvement. He wrote Team Two's score of 15 on the board and declared Team One the winner.

"We've covered a lot of ground today. Thanks for your participation and I'll see all of you tomorrow at eight a.m. sharp," Ben said, concluding the first day of the seminar.

12

After John left the seminar, he stopped at a sporting goods store and purchased a pedometer. When he arrived at ATMI, the first thing he did was track down Craig Green, who was a foreman on second shift.

"Craig, hope you have your walking shoes on," John said.

"Will sneakers do?" Craig asked. "Where am I walking?"

"I want you to take this pedometer," John said reaching into the sack and handing Craig the pedometer, "And start at the receiving dock for Part 2144. I want you to track the exact mileage that Part 2144 covers while it's in the shop."

"That's easy," Craig said. "It comes into receiving…"

"No. I don't want you to tell me what happens but rather where it goes. I want you to actually track the mileage by walking it. Make every single stop and go every place that part goes from the moment it arrives here until it's shipped to the customer."

"Sure, John, but why?"

"You know that Tuck and I are taking this seminar over at Aeroquip. One of the points the trainer brought home today was excessive motion as a form of waste. I watched a video that showed a part traveling five miles within four days. I'm afraid the same thing's happening here."

"Excessive motion? If the part has to be moved from place to place as part of the process, how can that be called excessive?"

"If we're taking unnecessary steps, if we're not moving things efficiently and that's a broad category, we're suffering waste which translates into costs. Think of a backyard barbeque. How many unnecessary trips do you make back to the kitchen to get the things you forgot?"

"Seems like you're splitting hairs. It's walking. What's the big deal?"

"Nothing if it's the barbeque, but if we're moving parts too much, it's taking time and that costs us. Let me tell you a story you've probably already heard but bear with me. When I was a teenager, I started counting my money every Sunday night. I always knew to the nickel how much money I had. It became a very important ritual for me. I kept that up for years. A couple of decades later, I'm the owner of a business that's both debt-free and profitable."

"Counting your nickels is your secret to success, huh?" Craig asked.

"Not the counting, but the principle behind the counting. That awareness. I've lost that acute awareness somewhere along the way. I'm going to regain it and I think Lean manufacturing might be exactly the ticket. Something else we're going to do is a Lean assessment. That's a purely objective view of how our business operates and it points out both strengths and weaknesses."

"How's Tuck taking all this?"

"Ask him about making paper airplanes the next time you see him," John answered. "Back to the task at hand, please track Part 2144. I just invested $ 20.00 in that pedometer and want to get my money's worth."

"Sure, John. Whatever makes you happy."

"Whatever makes us profitable is more accurate," John said, as he walked away from a somewhat befuddled Craig.

John left the shop and went out to his favorite rock. The sun was setting and softening the edges of the day. He mulled over the significant emotional changes he was going through and wondered if this is what they meant about a mid-life crisis. His marriage of twenty years was ending. Thank heavens it was ending with no rancor but a relatively amicable parting of two lives that had gone in different directions. His business partner of fifteen years wanted out. Again, fates were on his side since his business partner was a minority stock holder which gave John more leverage. His CPA was telling him to get out of the business he'd started with his life savings. As if all that wasn't enough, his doctor was advising back surgery.

He said aloud, "A great flame follows a little spark." *"Who had said that?"* he wondered. He snapped his fingers, remembering it was a quote from Dante.

In the distance, he heard a mournful howl. He instantly knew it was not the baying of a dog while hunting, having sighted his quarry. No, this was something entirely different. He listened carefully and heard the howl again. It emanated from the woods on the north side of the field. Without hesitation, he immediately started toward the baleful, almost pitiful, crying. He thought of Jimmy's beagle pup and was frightened that the dog had been hurt. Tramping through the underbrush, he paid no mind to his aching back but pressed forward, making his way toward the sound. When the dog fell silent, John shouted "Profit" and was rewarded with a mournful howl in response. He went into the woods, still needing the dog's cries as a homing device. A hundred feet into the woods, he spotted the beagle and realized he'd been right. The pup was hurt.

He dashed over to the dog and quickly sized up the situation. The dog had gotten tangled in a woven wire fence, his collar caught in the wires. Clearly from the dog's struggle to free himself, he'd only become more entwined and John saw that he was so bound up in the fence that his paws barely touched the ground.

John knelt down beside the pup, offering soft words of comfort, as he tried to disentangle the beagle. "This is a mess you've gotten yourself into, Profit," he softly said. Realizing the only way to free him was to cut his collar, John withdrew a pocket knife and quickly slit the collar.

The puppy whimpered, and licked John's hand. John petted the puppy's head as he absent-mindedly tucked the collar and pocket knife into his pants pocket.

John picked up the pup. The beagle was shaking, very frightened, but didn't seem to be seriously injured. John could feel the pup's racing heartbeat as he held him close and headed back toward the shop.

Once back at the shop, still with the pup in his arms, he crossed the manufacturing floor, heading toward his office. Employees stopped their work to watch him although John wasn't aware of the attention he was receiving.

When he'd reached his office, he carefully let the pup out of his arms. The beagle was still trembling but not nearly so bad as when John first found him. Going to the credenza, he poured water into a coffee cup and set it down. The pup greedily guzzled the water down and John knew he'd been caught in that fence for some time. After drinking as much as he could get out of the cup, he pawed the cup, knocking it over.

John didn't want to risk giving him too much but poured more water into the coffee cup. The dog lapped half a cup down, stepped back from the water, and burped.

"Now to get a hold of Jimmy," John thought. Remembering the collar, he dug it out of his pants pocket. Luckily, the collar had a tag. One side of the tag had a telephone number and the other had the word PROPHET on it.

"Prophet?" John thought. "I'll be damned," he said. "I thought Profit was a funny name for a dog but Prophet?"

Prophet cocked his head sideways and looked at John, his liquid brown eyes filled with gratitude.

"Prophet, your owner must be worried sick. I'll call him," John said and sat down at his desk. He dialed the telephone number on the tag. When Joyce McAlvey answered, John explained the situation and she said they'd be right over.

Good to her word, within minutes, Joyce and Jimmy were shown to John's office by Craig.

Hearing his master's voice, Prophet dashed from behind John's desk to Jimmy's waiting arms. Jimmy was puffy-eyed and his lower lip trembled when he first saw Prophet and grabbed him up, squeezing the very life out of him.

"John, thank you," Joyce said. "He's been gone since last night and we were all worried sick."

"What happened?" John asked. "Did he run away?"

"It's all my fault," Jimmy blurted out. "I got this new collar for him and put it on him yesterday when I got home from school. He pawed at it, didn't like it at all but I thought he'd get used to it. I went in to do my homework and he disappeared," he finished in a rush. "It's all my fault. You'll never have to wear a collar again, Prophet," Jimmy said directly to the puppy squirming in his arms.

"A collar's a good idea," John said, "Personally, I prefer the break-away kind so if he gets caught up on a fence again, when he tries to free himself, the collar will break free."

"No. He's never going to have to wear a collar again," Jimmy said.

Looking at Joyce for guidance, John waited until her gaze met his and she nodded, encouraging John to speak.

"It wasn't the collar. It was…" John searched for exactly the right words. "He needed some help with the change, that's all. We all need help with change, for that matter. We all get lost. He could get lost again and his tag on his collar could help get him home."

"How can a good thing have been so bad?" Jimmy asked.

"Sometimes it happens that way. That's why we really need to think about change and work through it carefully." He looked at Craig.

"That's right, Jimmy," Craig said. "We're going to be making some changes around here and we have to be careful, too. Like you do, with Prophet."

"Speaking of that," John said, looking at Joyce. "Jimmy said you named him. When I first heard the name, I thought it was P R O F I T. It wasn't until I saw his tag that I realized it was Prophet. Kind of an unusual name, isn't it?"

"We originally named him Buckles but he never answered to that. Besides, Prophet's been a prophet for me about Jimmy since the first day. I can tell that when he acts a certain way, I know Jimmy will be home within ten minutes. I can tell by his bark whether they're playing and having fun or if something's wrong. He's like an early warning system so Prophet seemed appropriate."

"I can see that," John said. "I could tell by his howl that something was wrong and that's why I tracked him down."

"Thank you," Joyce said to John. Tousling Jimmy's hair, she said to him, "Let's head for home, sport. I'll bet you're both hungry."

John and Craig walked Joyce and Jimmy with Prophet still in his arms to the front door.

"I got your message in there," Craig said. "Part 2411 travels around two and a half miles at a minimum. I began following Part 2411 and at the fourth work station, some parts went one way and some went the other because they needed rework. I took the shorter course because my feet were getting tired. I had no idea."

"I was afraid of that but now that we know it, we can do something about it," John said.

"How'd it happen?" Craig asked. "No one ever meant for that part to travel that far, especially when it's so unnecessary."

"We made changes and didn't watch what we were doing. This time, it'll be different," John said.

13

Tuesday morning, Ben started the seminar by showing the following quote on the computer screen:

> New opinions are always suspect,
> and usually opposed,
> without any other reason but because
> they're not already common.
>
> John Locke

"I use this slide as a reminder to all of us how easy it is to get locked into our paradigms. Reflect on yesterday's exercise. Did it meet your expectations? Or did things go differently than you'd thought they would? As we look at new ideas, please remember John Locke and his theory on new opinions." Ben gave the group a moment to ponder what he'd said before continuing.

"Today," he said, "We're going to be looking at our products in a new way. I'm encouraging everyone to keep an open mind. We're going to be looking at value-added, non-value-added and value stream mapping."

"The only good stream is the one with the trout," Rudy said, laughing uproariously at his own joke.

"You know, you mean that as a joke but there's a lot of truth in what you say. How much time would you spend fishing in a river that didn't have any trout?"

John quietly observed Ben and was impressed with his ability to take objections or distractions and use them as teaching aids.

"If you had the choice between one stream that was chock-full of trout and another one where the trout was much more scarce, you'd obviously stay at the first stream," Ben continued. "In a way, that's what value stream mapping is all about. It's a visual tool to help you recognize, identify and eliminate all forms of waste while maximizing effectiveness and efficiencies in the process. But, before we get into value stream mapping, I want us to spend some time with value-added and non-value-added functions."

"I don't know what you mean by value-added and non-value-added," Tuck said.

"Most people don't," Ben said. "We tend to assume that whatever we do in the manufacturing process is necessary to manufacture the product. But, is that what our customers are paying us for?"

"If it's necessary to the manufacturing process, wouldn't the customer naturally be paying for it?" Tuck asked.

"Not if they have a choice. Let me give you an example. Let's say you want to buy an ice cream cone. The first place has a good connection with a local ice cream supplier and their transportation costs are much lower than the second place. Hence, the first place will sell the same ice cream cone for less money. As the consumer, you're not going to tolerate higher prices because they have to pay higher transportation costs, are you? You, as the consumer, are going to buy at the first place—same ice cream cone for less money is a better value for you. The second place sees they're losing business and knows they have to do something, so they start offering three different sizes of ice cream cones, two different types of cones—waffle cones and plain, as well as frozen ice cream on a stick and ice cream sundaes. They've increased their elements of value-added by increasing what they do to the ice cream. Where are you most likely to buy an ice cream cone now?"

Tuck thought for a second and said, "If I was by myself, probably still at the first place, but if I had my family with me, I'd go to the second place because of the variety. More choices to satisfy more tastes."

"Good answer. Now, what if the second place offered exactly the amount of ice cream you desired?"

"What do you mean?" Tuck asked.

"Ever thrown away the uneaten portion of ice cream because it was too much for your tastes at that moment? Or, ever wished the ice cream cone had been a bit larger because after eating it, you still wanted more?"

"Sure."

"High on their success, the second place now offers "the right amount" ice cream cone. As a customer, you get to tell them exactly how much ice cream you want. Now, where would you go if you were alone?"

"I'd go to the second place, unless I was really broke. They're offering me more. I like having the choices."

"How 'bout we get back to the real world?" Rudy said impatiently.

Ben looked at Rudy, taking a long moment to study him before saying, "Starbucks' net revenue went up 23% from 2001 to 2002. Is that real-world enough for you?"

"It's not real-world enough for me," Ramona said. "I've never been in a Star-bucks. So, I don't get it."

"Starbucks is a prime example of value-added. They took a basic cup of coffee and added value by letting customers get exactly what they want, everything from a latte to cappuccino, vanilla to orange to chocolate to hazelnut flavoring. One of my favorites, by the way," Ben said. "People are paying five dollars for a cup of coffee at Starbucks. Not only that, they're standing in lines to do it. What would you do if your local restaurant tried to charge you five dollars for a cup of coffee?"

"What in tarnation does coffee have to do with manufacturing?" Rudy retorted.

Lucy said, "I guess the rumor's true that people still do live in caves in Texas. Can't you see what he's saying? I liken it to my hairdresser. I'm not paying her for her supplies, her shop or new scissors. I'm paying her to shape my hair."

"That's it!" John said with great enthusiasm. "Our customers pay us to shape metal. Period. They don't pay is to haul it in, store it or to ship it to them. They pay us to shape it. Everything we're doing has to be focused on that."

"You've taken a quantum leap here, John," Ben said. "In a nutshell, what you said is exactly what this seminar is all about. Everything we're discussing are tools to accomplish maximizing effectiveness. That's what value-added and non-value-added is all about. The flip side is cutting waste. It startles most people when they realize that value-added activities are rarely, if ever, over 5% of the whole picture. Ninety-five percent of our activities are in the non-value-added category. That's why both approaches have to be taken. Maximizing effectiveness in the value-added areas, such as concentrating on core competencies while simultaneously eliminating waste through the Lean principles."

"I couldn't believe the video of Petey Part yesterday," John said. "I thought you'd exaggerated to make your point. But, I had one of our supervisors measure how far a part travels at ATMI and it averaged out to two and a half miles. Our plant's not that big. The part must be backtracking like a drunk squirrel."

The participants laughed at John's expression and the tension in the room eased up a bit.

After lunch, the seminar participants began reconvening in the meeting room. Tuck got there ahead of everyone else and was busily making notes when Ben and Paul returned from lunch.

Looking around the room, Paul said, "Where's John?"

"He's not coming back," Tuck said, not looking up from the notes he was writing.

Hearing Tuck's words, Ben pulled up a chair and sat down next to Tuck.

"What happened?" Ben asked.

"I thought he was really on board," Paul said, looking crestfallen.

Tuck looked up to see the incredibly worried looks on their faces.

"Maybe it's not a totally lost cause," Paul said. "At least, he's letting you stay."

"Letting me stay?" Tuck asked. "I'm under the strictest orders not to miss a single second of this seminar. In fact, John wants to know if it's okay if I tape record the rest of the sessions."

"Now, I'm totally confused. John bolts on the seminar but wants you to tape record it. I've already told him that commitment from the top is crucial. No offense, Tuck, but he has to be on-board with this to make it work at ATMI."

"You think he's not on-board?" Tuck asked.

"He's not here," Paul said.

Tuck paused a second, then said, "No, he's not here. But, he's not here because he's back at ATMI implementing Lean as we speak."

14

Before dawn, John was wandering around ATMI. At this early hour, the building was eerily silent.

While Tuck stayed at the Aeroquip seminar, John had immersed himself in the local library, reading everything he could on Lean manufacturing. Everything he read hailed Lean as a means of increasing profitability by reducing waste. He knew in his gut that Lean made all the sense in the world for ATMI. But, as he looked around the shop, he realized that attending a seminar and reading books was a far cry from the actual transition involving flesh and blood people. He wondered, seriously wondered, how his employees would react to this radical change. Most of his employees had been with ATMI for a good amount of time and they were competent machinists. Now, to tell them everything was going to change? *"Not everything,"* John reminded himself. Customer service had always been crucial to ATMI and that wasn't going to change, other than to get better.

He and Tuck had put together a strategy over a long Sunday brunch yesterday. They were going to meet with the key employees today to announce the change to Lean manufacturing. This meeting was not going to be a debate about whether they should go Lean. That decision had already been made, but he wanted everyone on board and wanted their input to make the transition as painless as possible.

As he walked around the shop, he marveled at the quiet. Like still sentries, the equipment stood in silent attention, waiting for the arrival of the warriors. In less than an hour, people would start arriving and shortly thereafter, the machines would be humming. Everything he'd read about Lean emphasized how important top level commitment was to the Lean transformation and he was committed. Now to get everyone else to share his enthusiasm.

"I am committed," John said aloud.

"Or you should be committed," Tuck said, surprising John.

"I didn't hear you come in," John said. "Why are you here so early?"

"I guess, like you're doing, I wanted a look at the good, ole' days before we usher in the new order of business."

"How do you think they'll take it?"

"Honestly? I think they're going to squall like scalded cats."

"That's encouraging," John said sarcastically.

"You asked. We're going to turn their world upside down. Yes, I know it's good for the company and good for them, but we're putting them on a roller coaster ride and they didn't buy a ticket."

"It's my company," John said.

"That's another thing that concerns me. Your attitude."

"Mine?" John asked, incredulous.

"John, you're like a wagon train master in the old west. We're all in our Conestoga wagons and have followed you across the prairie. We've battled Indians before, always circling the wagons and fighting it out. Now, here comes trouble again and instead of circling the wagons, you're bringing in a whole new strategy. It's bound to freak them out."

"Are you getting cold feet, Tuck?"

"No. I'm trying to caution you about how you approach people."

"Spit it out."

"John, you're strong, tough, competent and can be intimidating. People will follow you simply because it's you and that's a good thing. But, in this transformation, we're trying to achieve high independence on the part of the people. They have to buy into this because they believe it's the right thing to do, not just because you said so."

"Point taken," John said.

As John and Tuck had been talking, the shop was slowly coming to life. Employees were filing in, after punching in, and heading for their work stations. John went up to the mezzanine and looked out over the shop floor. He noticed a pattern of employees coming in and going to their supervisors to get their instructions. He cupped his chin in his hand as he leaned over the railing observing the morning rituals that had gone on for two decades. A couple of supervisors had a line of employees waiting for instructions. He'd seen this same thing for years but was now seeing it with new eyes.

What a waste, he thought. His employees were bright. They had good minds, good attitudes, top-notch skills, yet, they needed to get their marching orders before putting those talents to work. He glanced at his watch. It was taking a good fifteen minutes to get people even headed in the right direction to work. His brow furrowed as he did a quick calculation of forty or so employees multiplied by fifteen minutes of waste.

After all of the employees were finally at work, productive work as John saw it, he headed toward the conference room. This meeting would be key. He'd invited all of the top management through first line supervisors to share the vision of Lean.

Everyone in the conference room fell silent when John walked in.

"Is everyone here?" John asked.

"Who'd be late to this meeting?" Luke Adams, third shift supervisor, asked. "We hear the place is closing."

"Closing?" John said, clearly surprised by Luke's comment.

"Sure. You know how it is on third shift. Just rumors but this one's been pretty strong."

"It may be strong but it's wrong. We're not closing," John said. "What on earth…oh, never mind. Let's get on with it. The purpose of this meeting is to discuss how we're going to transform ATMI from traditional manufacturing to Lean manufacturing. Tuck and I attended a seminar at Aeroquip and have decided that Lean manufacturing makes all the sense in the world for ATMI. Tuck is going to review the fundamental principles of Lean and after that, we're going to lay out a plan for implementation." John sat down, turning the meeting over to Tuck.

The group patiently listened to Tuck's explanation of the Lean manufacturing philosophy. In summing up, Tuck said, "Lean is a means of reducing waste, streamlining production and improving quality. It's what we have to do to compete. I'm sure you all have questions so let's get those answered before we start the planning."

"It won't work here," Frank Cazzlone, ATMI Quality Manager said. He stood up and poured himself a second cup of coffee. "It's a great philosophy, I suppose, but it's not something we can do."

"Why do you say that?" Tuck asked.

"Lean manufacturing is something all of the quality experts are familiar with and it's been dictated by what's happening in automotive. The Big Three are nailing their suppliers for cost reductions while demanding increases in improvements. They're using Lean and have offered Lean to us as a means to meet their demands but we don't have their resources. It's a Trojan horse."

"What do the quality experts say about Lean?" Tuck asked.

"They think it's wonderful for the big guys. But, there's no proof it'll work for a small job shop or even a medium-sized manufacturer."

"What's your biggest concern?" John asked.

"Quality, of course. Do you think Aeroquip is going to smile sweetly when they receive junk from us simply because we're Lean? Not a chance."

"What on earth makes you think we'll be shipping junk?" John asked.

"I knew it the second Tuck said operators would be responsible for their own quality. Getting rid of inspectors is rubbish. In fact, John, that's something I want to discuss with you after this meeting. We actually need to increase our number of inspectors."

"I'm with Frank," Newton Nestor said. "As the tool crib manager, I know how these people abuse things and I spend half my day running down missing tools. They break them and try to hide it. They lose them or maybe steal them. They don't give a rip about the tools. They're not going to give a rip about producing good parts."

"Exactly," Frank said. "Without someone riding their butts, they'll be shipping junk and we will be out of business then."

"Hold up a second," Tuck said. "Employees want to do a good job. Who comes to work planning on making junk? That doesn't make sense."

"I didn't say they plan on making junk. I said that's what they'll be shipping if there's no one to inspect their work. We're in contact with the customers and know what they're expecting. The operators don't know that."

"Yeah," Luke Adams, third shift supervisor, said. "We think we're doing a good job until an inspector rejects everything."

"See?" Frank said.

"Don't interrupt me," Luke said. "We're told to produce parts to certain specifications and we do it. Then, some inspector comes along and rejects them. Most of the time, we're not even told why they're being rejected. It's no wonder Frank thinks we're producing junk. It wouldn't be that way if everyone knew the standards or when they're changed."

"It won't be that way with Lean," Tuck said. "Everyone will know the standards."

"So you expect my inspectors to become messenger boys?" Frank asked sarcastically. "Pretty high priced talent for messenger boys, don't you think?"

John noticed Tuck's jaw muscles clenching and knew they were in for another round of production versus quality if he didn't intercede.

"Take a fifteen minute break," John said.

When no one moved from their seats, John said, "Take fifteen minutes now. Only fifteen minutes, though. We have a lot of planning to do."

Almost reluctantly, hating to miss the fight brewing, people slowly got up and left the room.

John took Tuck aside.

"Don't get drawn into that battle, Tuck," John coached. "Frank's afraid of losing territory and he's right. His department will lose some of their cop-like authority and all he's doing is trying to protect his turf."

Tuck was still steaming and took a few deep breaths to relax.

"What the hell is wrong with him?" Tuck said. "Doesn't he see that Lean is good for everyone? He's a selfish bastard."

"Taking the bait won't help," John said. "I'll handle it when everyone gets back."

15

When everyone reassembled after the break, John took the floor.

"I may not have been clear at the beginning of this meeting," John said. "The decision to go Lean has already been made. This meeting is not about whether we're going to go Lean or not. That decision has been made. We are going Lean. This meeting is about planning how we go Lean. Are we all perfectly clear on this point?"

In response to John's proclamation, Newton puffed up like an adder while Frank sat still and silent as a stone statue. Their reactions were mentally noted by John.

John continued, "The first order of business is to define our Core Competencies." Core competencies are defined as our key areas of production strength. By that, I mean products that we can routinely produce to the highest customer standard while maintaining a healthy return on our investment. Core competencies are what we consistently do best. As an example, would you expect to get a New York strip steak at McDonald's? Of course not. That's not one of their core competencies. Hamburgers, fries and milkshakes are part of their core competencies."

He glanced around the room to see if anyone had any questions before continuing.

"Too often in the past, we've taken on jobs that were out of our range of our core competencies and it's cost us dearly. That's stopping now."

"What about the customer requests that come in that don't meet our core competencies?" Larry Myers, ATMI Sales Manager, asked.

"We have three options. First, can we sub-contract the work out? Second, can the new product become a new core competency for us? Third, we refuse the work," John answered.

"Refuse the work?" Larry asked, looking as if he'd just been told that apple pie was no longer American.

"Larry, I know this is different from the way we've done things in the past, but it is a crucial part of becoming Lean," John said.

"Different? It sounds like a prescription for disaster," Larry responded.

"Just the opposite. Taking on work that is out of our core competencies is a prescription for disaster."

"Come on, Larry," Tuck chimed in. "You remember that last 'special' job we did for Skyline? We lost our butts and John damned near fractured his foot from kicking the machine so many times. No one was happy. We produced a barely acceptable part that Skyline reluctantly accepted, not to mention we didn't make a dime."

"I'm concerned about losing customers," Larry said. "We're not in the business of saying 'No.' Our customers have come to depend on us to do anything they've asked."

"Would you ask your dentist to take out your gall bladder?" John asked.

"Uhh, no. Not unless my gall bladder was in a really weird spot," Larry said. The ensuing laughter helped ease the tension in the room.

"That's the point," John said. "It means we're going to have to be very conscious about educating our customers. This also really means that we're going to be able to live up to the promises we've routinely made to our customers."

"I don't get that," Larry said, looking confused.

"We've taken on projects because our customers asked. They're depending on us for our professional expertise. When we agree to produce a part that's not a core competency, we're jeopardizing the quality we can send to them as well as creating a world of frustration for our own people, not to mention that we don't make any money doing this. In the future, when we say 'Yes', we're going to be able to deliver them a quality product, on time, at a reasonable cost, that makes us money without all of the unnecessary frustration."

"I don't know about this, John," Ron Stabler, first shift supervisor, said. "It sounds like you don't have confidence in our abilities. That's not going to go well with the guys on the floor."

"You mean the operators would rather break their necks trying to produce a foreign part?" John asked.

"You're missing the key point," Ron said. "There's always a learning curve. Sure, the first time we produce a new part, it's a nightmare but that's true every time we do something new. Call it human nature or whatever. But, that's how we learn. By cutting off new products, you're cutting off growth. How are we going to expand if we say 'No' all the time? Besides, back to the guys on the floor, they're capable of doing anything. This message will tell them that you think they can't cut it anymore."

"How do the rest of you feel?" John asked.

The people in the room, with the exception of Tuck, murmured assent to what Ron and Larry were saying.

"This is going to be more difficult than I realized," thought John, followed about a more troubling concern. *"What if they're right?"*

"I don't claim to be an expert in Lean," John said. "Tuck and I attended the Lean seminar at Aeroquip and made the decision that ATMI was going to go Lean. We were given a roadmap or a transformation map of how to get ATMI there and the starting point is determining our core competencies." He glanced at his watch.

"This isn't going to happen overnight," he said. "What I want everyone to do today is watch very carefully how our production goes. Make notes of both the positives and negatives. I'm especially interested in finding the parts that we produce easily and competently and the parts that cause us all the headaches. In fact, I want you to bring in parts that we do well, meaning high quality, on time and profitably, and bring in parts that cost us in terms of lack of profitability, aggravation and frustration. We'll meet again tomorrow to continue our discussion."

After everyone but Tuck and John had left the room, John closed the door.

"Well, that was fun," John said.

"Frank's going to be a real problem," Tuck said. "He's so fired up about losing his authority that he can't see how this is going to be good for all of us."

"Tuck, he raised some good questions and I agree that he's doing a major bit of turf protection. The crucial point is that every operator will have to be trained to be responsible and accountable for their own quality. They've depended on quality for so long and we're ripping away their safety nets."

"Safety nets, hell," Tuck said. "We're ripping away their chains. John, you don't know what it's like on the floor in terms of morale. An operator will produce a good part or what he thinks is a good part. The first inspector says 'No,' and if the operator protests and gets a second inspector, the second inspector is just as likely to say 'Yes.' Then, we call Frank, the Grand Poobah, and wait, and wait and wait, until he finally decides to show up and give us his ruling. He never bothers to explain why he's ruling one way or another. However, and this is just my suspicion, he rules using other criteria than the customer's standards, like which inspector he favors or what kind of mood he's in. I swear to God, I've had the same part both rejected and passed by him on the same day. Now you explain that to me."

"What are you suggesting?"

"That he plays God. John, I hate to admit this, but I've tricked him a couple of times. I've taken parts he's rejected, given them to another operator and gotten a second ruling, more often passing than not, depending on the operator and the inspector."

"Paul said we'd run into problems that we didn't know about."

"That you didn't know about," Tuck said.

"Fair enough. With Lean, all of the skeletons are going to come out of the closet. Paul also said we'd probably lose people. I know you'll keep this in confidence but I think we better start looking for another Quality Manager. Based on what you've said and his attitude, I don't think he'll stick around."

"What about Nestor?"

"Nestor will be fine. He's frustrated. He keeps losing tools and I'm always chewing his tail about the expenses in his department. He's not trying to protect turf. The increased accountability by the operators is something he's been wanting for a long time. He just doesn't see that Lean is the way to go yet but he will."

"Okay. Are you concerned about the attitudes of the others?"

"Not really," John said, trying to convince himself more than Tuck. "This is a major change and that's frightening for people. We just have to find the best strategy to help people cope with their fears while embracing Lean. I don't know what was on your schedule today but I'd like you to ride shotgun on everyone to make sure they're collecting information on the good and bad parts. We have to settle this core competency question before we move on."

At the end of the day, John slipped out of ATMI and headed for home. As he pulled out of the driveway, something caught his eye. He glanced to the left and saw Prophet's rump. Just the pup's wriggling rump was visible from the drainage ditch beside the road.

Wondering what kind of trouble Prophet had gotten himself into now, John pulled his car over to the side of the road and stopped.

Mightily focused on his own work, Prophet didn't pay attention as John carefully walked up to him.

Prophet had the leg of a dead deer firmly grasped in his jaws and was trying to pull the entire carcass of the deer with all his might. First, he'd tug to the right, then, to the left, managing to not move the hundred pound carcass an inch.

As if it would help, Prophet began growling; the throaty, muffled growl of a frustrated pup with his mouth full.

John squatted down at the edge of the drainage ditch about three feet away from Prophet.

"Prophet," he said. "Hey, boy, come here."

Prophet didn't respond until John had called him the third time.

Very reluctantly, Prophet let go of the deer's leg and turned toward John.

"It's just too big for you, boy," John said.

Prophet wheeled toward the deer carcass with renewed vengeance and tore into its leg, violently shaking his head.

John picked up his cell phone and called Tuck at ATMI. While waiting for Tuck to arrive, John watched Prophet exhaust himself on the carcass.

When Tuck drove up, he walked up to John, carrying an axe.

"I'm sure there's a good reason why you wanted an axe," Tuck said. "Should've known it would involve the mutt," he said affectionately.

"I don't know how Prophet's family is going to feel about this, but a beagle is a hunter and his efforts shouldn't go unrewarded. He'll tire out pretty quickly then, we can help him."

As though he'd heard John's words, Prophet released the deer's leg, backed up a few paces and sat down. He cocked his head first to the right, then left, as if trying to figure out what to do now.

Tuck took a step toward the carcass and, sensing his approach, Prophet lunged at the deer, grabbing the leg again with renewed vigor. Growling all the while, he tore furiously but futilely, violently shaking his head.

"Moved a bit too soon there, Tuck," John said.

"Like that dog's ever going to drag that deer anywhere. All I wanted to do was help him," Tuck said.

"Remind you of anyone?"

"Now who would I know that would remind me of a dog attacking a deer ten times his size?"

"Frank."

"Huh?" Tuck said, surprised.

"Same principle. What Prophet is showing us is the same principle we saw with Frank. Heavy-duty turf protection. It's his deer and no one's going to take it until he's good and ready to let it go. Prophet taught me another lesson today. We have good people at ATMI and I've always tried to listen to their input. I may have listened too much today. I almost bought their arguments about the core competencies issues. Paul Conner told me a story about why Northside went out of business. They had over three million dollars in new business but couldn't deliver because it was the wrong business. Apparently, they were well outside of their core competencies. The message to us is that we've been lucky."

"What does luck have to do with any of this?"

"When a customer has asked us for a part, we've done our damnedest to produce it, often at cost or worse, the part cost us more than we could charge for it.

While we were dumping resources into parts that were out of our core competencies, our main business, our true core competencies, had to be suffering. We were lucky we didn't take a dive. It's just like Prophet. If he'd found a dead rabbit or squirrel, he'd be able to handle it. But a deer? So he's burning up precious energy trying to drag home something he can't even move an inch."

John snapped his fingers and whistled softly to get Prophet's attention.

"Here, boy," he called. "Prophet. Come here. Prophet."

Clearly getting tired, Prophet released the deer's leg and glanced at John. He looked back at the deer and howled piteously.

"He's calling in the rest of his pack and that's us," John said. Walking slowly toward Prophet, he gently called his name. When he was about five feet from the pup, he squatted down and called the pup again.

Prophet trotted over to John and in frustration and exhaustion, dropped down beside John.

"Good boy," John said, rubbing the pup's head. He gently picked the pup up and headed toward his car.

"Tuck, chop off the lower part of that leg and wrap it in something. Throw it in the trunk of my car and I'll let Prophet have it when I get him home. Get somebody out here to get rid of that carcass."

"John, you're such a strong animal rights activist and don't even hunt. I'm surprised…"

"Surprised that I'd help a hound be a hound? Nothing I'd ever do would make Prophet a vegetarian but I can help him be the best hunter he can be."

As John situated both himself and Prophet in the front seats of his car and popped the truck release, Tuck quickly dispatched his job and slammed the trunk down.

As John drove away, he thought pensively that Prophet's problem with trying to eat the deer all at once was like instituting Lean at ATMI. It'd be a lot easier on everyone to eat the deer one bite at a time instead of choking on one big gulp.

16

When everyone arrived the next morning, they found John in the conference room. The entire table was covered with parts produced by ATMI and there were two small but different-sized buckets on the end of the conference table. John was methodically picking up a part and either placing it in one of the two buckets or throwing it into a ever-growing pile of parts in the corner.

People filled their cups with coffee and were milling around the conference table, so engrossed in John's activities that no one spoke. As Tuck walked in, he heard someone say, "The old man has really lost it."

Taking in the scene in a glance, Tuck said, "Okay, everyone take a seat. Let's get started. It looks like we have some catching up to do." Not quite sure what John was doing, but having confidence in John, he sat down as if this was just the normal beginning of any staff meeting.

John continued placing parts in one of the three locations, one of the buckets or in the pile in the corner, until everyone had sat down.

"I don't like the way yesterday's meeting went at all," John said. "There's a lot we have to do and very little time to do it in. I said it yesterday and I'll say it again, hopefully, for the last time. ATMI is going Lean. That is not open for discussion. However, one of the major thrusts of Lean is people working together as a team, not just managers and supervisors telling employees what to do, so in that spirit, I want everyone's input on the best way to bring Lean into ATMI."

"Whatever you say, John," Ron Stabler said. "But, what's with all the parts?"

"It's the method I've selected for determining which parts we'll continue to produce and to establish parts families."

"Oh, that's right up there with astrology for a decision-making process," said Frank Cazzlone, the Quality Manager.

John glared at him.

"You know, Frank, you might inquire before jumping to conclusions," John said.

"I'm not jumping to conclusions. The best way for us to determine which parts we're going to continue making should be what our customers want from us. It's what we do best. What you're doing is playing tiddly winks."

A deadly silence fell over the room.

John picked up a few more parts and sorted them before responding.

Finally, he said, "I very much want this to be an open forum for discussion but we will show respect for others' viewpoints."

"That's a great idea," said Luke Adams, third shift supervisor. "Frank, you may not realize it but you jump to conclusions all the time about what third shift does. Like when…"

John cut him off. "This isn't the time, Luke. Besides, when we have Lean implemented, every operator will know, and I mean know, what the quality standards are and what they have to do to hit them. They'll be calling the shots."

Frank snorted.

"John," Tuck said, "Can you explain how you're using the buckets?"

"Sure. Frank made a good point about us concentrating on what we do best but I'm not sure he was looking at the right criteria. It was so obvious to me last night watching Prophet tangle with that deer carcass. Using him as the example, someone could determine which prey is best for him by measuring his weight, body strength and agility, jaw span and structure of his teeth. Now, that beagle may want to take down every deer in the forest or be instructed to attack a wild boar, but he'd fail. It's the same with us. Looking at our parts, we've invested a great deal in machinery and operator training to make the parts that fit in these two buckets. Those parts," he motioned to the pile in the corner, "don't fit. And the majority of the time we stepped out of our boundaries of what we do best, it's cost us dearly. So, from this point forward, we're only going to produce parts that fit in one of these two buckets. Everything else we'll either sub-contract or we'll refuse."

"By God, John, I see what you're talking about," Tuck said, clearly surprised by his own developing awareness. "This is making sense to me. The machining, the raw parts…everything fits into…fits into one of the buckets."

"I'll grant you it's not the most orthodox method of doing this," John said, "But this will establish our core competencies. We maximize our effectiveness by concentrating on our core competencies and we don't do anything that doesn't fall within those parameters. I'd like everyone here to help me determine the future of these parts."

Tentatively at first, the group began sorting through the parts, assigning them to the buckets or the floor. Once the parts had all been sorted, they were tagged and logged.

Luke, third shift supervisor, said, "Maybe it's because I'm normally asleep right now but this is making sense to me."

"You're asleep, like usual," Tuck said, laughing.

"Aw, thanks, Tuck. Always nice to count on you for a word of encouragement, but seriously, if you'll look at the pile of parts on the floor, those are the parts that have given us, well, at least third shift, nightmares. I always got the willies when I'd come in and see that one or more of these parts were on the operations orders. John, are you serious that we're done making these parts?"

"Yes."

"Then, I'm all for Lean!" Luke said.

"You're just trying to get out of work," Frank said, not smiling.

"Damn it, Frank. That's not fair. You're never here in the middle of the night when we're having trouble with one of these parts but you're sure here in the morning telling us everything we did wrong."

"Well, from what I understand about Lean, you won't have to worry about that. Everyone's going to get to make the quality decisions and then, you can all listen to the client when he calls to bitch."

"That assumes we'll be shipping junk," John said.

Frank shrugged his shoulders.

"Frank, you're going to play a critical part in the Lean process. It'll be up to you to train the operators in what is quality and what is not. By eliminating these parts, you'll have that many fewer parts to train. Your role is going to change dramatically from cop to coach," John said.

"Like I'm going to have time to train everyone before the customers cancel their orders and we're out of business."

"I certainly hope that's not the case," John said. "It'll take some planning which has to coordinate with which orders are the hottest."

"Frank, it also seems like separating the parts this way would make it easier. Obviously, parts in each bucket are similar to other parts in the same bucket," Tuck said.

"Yes, that's true. I suppose it would make it easier."

"Then," Tuck continued, "We have to develop our part families. That simply means grouping all the parts that are similar in size, shape, machining, tooling and workholding."

"I think the employees have more of an idea of what makes quality than we're giving them credit," Tuck said. "We've been in here most of the day with only a few interruptions. I think that's a pretty good sign. Speaking of employees, we're all set for Saturday."

"Good," John said.

"Saturday?" several people asked in unison.

"Yes, we've rented the auditorium and a meeting this Saturday is mandatory. We're going to introduce Lean to everyone at the same time so we're all on the same page," Tuck said.

"Frank," John said, "I'd like you to make a presentation on how we're going to train everyone on Saturday, too." John glanced at his watch. "We've done a lot here today but as Frank pointed out, we still have orders to fill so let's hit the floor. Luke, why don't you head for home and get some sleep."

After everyone had left the conference room except John and Tuck, John said, "What do you think?"

"I don't know. I saw some progress in Frank today but still..."

"I know. I want to give him every chance to do this but I can't let his negative attitude get in the way of our progress toward Lean. It's going to be his decision whether he's with us or not."

"Frank's always been on a power trip. I think that comment about 'cop to coach' really got to him. He's not going to like his power being stripped."

"In all fairness to him, though, he's had a huge responsibility in the past. He's the first one I nail if quality is bad. He's not going to lose power but just have it directed a new way. However, if he can't make the transition, that won't stop what we're doing. Paul said we could expect some people not to stay during this transition and Frank may be one of those people. That's why I'm gathering resumes."

"What about the rest?"

"I don't know. I think today was good because people really got an idea of our core competencies. While most people dislike change, I think they'll more readily accept it when they see clear benefits from the change. Lean will do that, I hope."

There was a soft knock on the conference door and Estelle stuck her head in.

"Sorry to disturb you, John, but that little boy is here to see you and he seems upset."

"Little boy?" John thought "Must be Jimmy," John said. "If he's upset, I wonder if something's happened to Prophet," John said, getting up from his seat and heading toward the lobby.

In the lobby, he found Jimmy, bleary-eyed and upset, with Prophet sniffing around the chairs.

"Hi, Jimmy. What's wrong?"

"They want to put him in a kennel," Jimmy said.

"Who does?"

"My folks. We're going on vacation for two weeks and they won't let me take Prophet. So, they're going to stick him in some old dumb kennel. He'll hate it."

"If it's only for two weeks…" John said, squatting down and scratching Prophet behind the ears.

"Oh, that's great!" Jimmy squealed. "I just knew you'd said 'Yes.' Mom said I shouldn't bother you with this but I just knew you'd let him stay with you." Jimmy beamed.

"I…uhhh…" John stammered.

Prophet rolled over on his back so John could scratch his tummy.

"Does your mom know you're here?" John finally asked.

"Yes. She finally gave in after I begged and begged her to let me ask you. She made me promise not to beg you so I didn't."

"This is really against my better judgment," John said, "But it's not the first time I've done that. Okay. He can stay with me. You'll have to give me a list of the food he's eating."

"Oh, no problem. I'll bring everything over," Jimmy said, and, on impulse, hugged John.

"When are you leaving?" John asked.

"Tomorrow."

"Great," thought John. *"I'm turning my company head over heels and now I'm puppy-sitting while I'm doing it."*

"All right. I'll stop by your house tonight and pick up Prophet then. It'll be around six o'clock."

"Oh, thanks so much. You're the best," Jimmy said. He and Prophet bounded out the front door of ATMI.

17

On Saturday morning, John arrived at the auditorium right after Tuck and Frank which was about an hour before the rest of the employees were to show up.

Tuck and Frank were busy making preparations for the presentation, getting their slides ready, making sure the sound system worked, adjusting the lighting.

"Hey, John, are you bringing pop corn?" Tuck asked.

They'd rented the old Regal movie theatre which had shown its last movie a month after the new multi-cinema complex had gone in.

The stage had heavy burgundy velvet draperies and the seats were covered in once-deep plush now thread-worn with age.

"Lots of memories of this place," John said. "Every Saturday afternoon, I came here to see the latest installment of Red Rider."

"Red Rider?" Tuck asked.

"Yes. It was a western that always ended in a cliff-hanger. It was the short clip before the actual show. Obviously before your time," Frank answered.

"You, too?" John asked Frank.

"Not here but it was the same where I grew up. Quarter a show, as I recall."

"A quarter?" Tuck said. "Hell, you can't go to the movies today without taking out a mortgage on your house."

"It was a quarter for the Saturday matinee. By the time I was dating, it was a buck for the evening feature," John said.

"A buck?" Tuck said, quite astonished.

"It seems like a long time ago."

"It was a long time ago," Frank said. "Everything changes, I suppose, but I'm not sure all of these changes are for the good."

"Right. Let's go back to the good, ole days when polio was a threat and measles could be life-threatening. That's the problem with too much of fondly remembering the good, old days. We forget the bad things. Besides, change is inevitable."

"John, are you sure you want to go through with this?" Frank asked.

"Are you serious?" John answered. "Hell, yes. We have to become more competitive and I think this is the best way to do it."

"It's a great approach," Paul Conner said, walking up from the back of the auditorium. "Thanks for inviting me. It would've been a lot easier on us at Aero-quip if we'd introduced Lean this way."

"We're glad you could make it," John said. "I'm sure there'll be questions we can't answer."

"Paul, do you really think Lean made that big of a difference?" Frank asked.

"Absolutely," Paul answered. "It was a huge change in culture for us but self-ishly, I have significantly more confidence that we're shipping quality parts on time and under budget to our customers."

"Frank, do you have the training matrix?"

"Yes, in full color slides in the PowerPoint presentation. Realistically, it'll take us about six months to have everyone cross-trained but we'll see increased flexibility in the operators within sixty days."

"Good," John said.

The employees began showing up at the theatre; some milling around, some taking their seats, and a few came up to the podium where John, Frank, Tuck and Paul were working.

When the entire group had taken their seats, John began the meeting.

"Sorry to disrupt your Saturday on such short notice, but we're going to be making changes at ATMI and I do mean 'we,' as in all of us. We're going to Lean. Now, it's my pleasure to turn the meeting over to Tuck."

Tuck went to the podium, took a sip of water and began.

"First, I want all of you to know that John and I have given this a lot of thought," Tuck began. "Some of you may be wondering why we've decided to go in, what may seem to you, as a radically different direction, when we've been so successful doing what we're doing now. That's a fair question. I think it's safe to say that John has not been successful all these years by following everybody else. He's built this business by having the vision to be one step ahead of the competition. In his best judgment, he feels this is the next step to take in growing the business. I think he's right.

"While Lean manufacturing may seem very different from what we're doing right now, it's really very simple. The whole idea is to reduce waste that costs us money, wherever we find it. It will also help us increase our flexibility, and decrease lead times that will make us more efficient and productive. Finally, we believe it will help us provide our customers with the highest quality possible." Tuck paused. "It will do this while dramatically reducing our operating costs." Tuck could see some people roll their eyes. He knew 'reducing costs' meant lay-offs and a cutback in resources to many people. He continued, "Don't get your panties all in a bunch. We're not going to reduce staff or cutback on the things that you need to do your job. But, we are going to work smarter.

"We'll accomplish it by using a number of Lean techniques," Tuck continued. "You eliminate waste by reducing overproduction, excessive transportation, waiting around for the next event to happen, excess motion in production, over processing, defects and inventory. First, we'll dramatically reduce inventory; both parts and material. Of course, we'll have to install inventory pull systems to monitor both more closely. Imagine our inventories like groceries at the supermarket. We'll also produce parts in work cells that will increase operator efficiency and make them responsible for quality."

Tuck paused as he looked around the room into stares that included a range from quizzical, to defiant. "Look people, I know this won't be easy for some of you. However, it will help us become stronger and more competitive. But, we can't do it without your support."

A voice from the back of the room boomed over the chatter. "I still don't see why we're disrupting everything that's made us successful."

John had been observing the reaction to Tuck's presentation quietly until now. "What makes you assume we're all that successful?" John asked. "I'm the guy that pays all the bills and I'm here to tell you that, if you measure success in dollars and cents, we're not as successful today as we were yesterday and we won't be as successful tomorrow as we are today, if things stay the same."

"If were not making as much money as we used to, maybe it's time to raise prices," another employee said.

"You don't understand," Tuck interrupted. "That's not the way it works anymore. It used to be, we would do exactly that. As our costs went up, we would pass them on to our customers. But, not any more. Now, when we get a new order from our customers, we agree upon a price for the first year and then they require a price reduction of 3-5% for each subsequent year after that. So, not only can't we raise the price, we have to reduce it, or we lose the business."

The room got quiet.

"You mean as our costs go up, we're required to reduce our prices? That's crazy," said someone in the back of the room. "You can't stay in business that way."

"You're beginning to get the picture," said Tuck. "We won't stay in business unless we can find ways to reduce our costs faster then we're required to reduce our prices. That's what this is all about. I know we all have a lot of fun here. We enjoy the work and each other. But, let's face it. We're not in business for an emotional experience. We're in business to make a profit."

18

Prophet bolted out of John's office with Estelle fast on his heels. He tore around the offices, dashing into each office and cubicle, making a fast circle, and back to the hall. His short legs were pumping like little pistons and his nose was to the ground, leading him on his search. Estelle was no match for the pup as he agilely dodged her attempts to catch him. Someone opened the door to the manufacturing floor and Prophet made a beeline for the open doorway, making in through a split second before Estelle yelled to shut the door.

Once on the manufacturing floor, Prophet grew more frenzied as he dashed down the corridors between the equipment. He didn't have quite the traction on the concrete floor as he had in the carpeted offices. Spying his quarry, he made a fast right turn and actually slid on his side, crashing into John's legs.

"Prophet!" John said.

"That's your answer?" Ty Ferren said. "Profit? That's why we're going through all these changes? Lean's all about profit?"

"No. Prophet's the name of the dog," John said, bending down to pet Prophet. The pup bounced up and down like a kid on Christmas morning. "We're going Lean to improve our operations, get rid of waste, improve quality and productivity. One of the benefits will be increased profit, though."

"Thought so," Ty said. "It's all about money."

"Now that you mention it," John said, "we're going to talk about money. I'm not going to bore you with the story of how I started this business and the risks I took. Instead, we're going to talk about what profit means for this company. I'm sick and tired of everyone thinking profit's a bad word. It's not. Without profit, we're out of business and you're out of a job."

"Well, yeah…"

"Well, yeah, nothing. It's true. There are lots of ways to cut costs in an operation, like cutting jobs. With Lean, increased profitability is one, and I stress, one of the benefits. But, it's a very important benefit. We're not sole supplier on orders. Very few customers are buying that way so every quote we get is part of a bid process. We're competing for every piece of business we get in here. Being able to meet our customers' demands in terms of quality, time and cost is absolutely crucial to our staying in business. As we discussed in the Saturday presentation, Aeroquip has required a three percent reduction in costs. That means we have to produce the same part for three percent less. How would you feel if I told everyone they were going to have a three percent reduction in their pay?"

"Uhhh…. I'd be looking for a job."

"Of course you would and I wouldn't blame you."

"Now that you mentioned money, I would like to talk to you about a raise."

"You've been here three years and every year, you've gotten a raise."

"Yeah. So what?"

"So what? Where do you think those raises are coming from? Employees expect to get raises and customers expect to pay less. We're facing greater competition both in the states and abroad. How do you think we're going to stay in business?"

Ty was silent.

"I'm glad, really glad, you brought up money. Profit. You have two kids, right? They're in high school?"

"Yes. Two boys."

"Are they planning on college?"

"Yes."

"How are you planning on paying for it?"

"I'm…well, we've put some money aside but it's going to be difficult. But I don't see what that has to do with Lean."

"It's really the same thing," John said. "To be able to provide for your kids' college education, you're going to have to make some changes, like savings, cutting back on some expenses, increasing your income, finding ways to make the dollar go farther. Right?"

"Yeah, right. Big time."

"You have to find a way of increasing and managing your personal profit, right?"

"Now I see what you're driving at," Ty said.

"Same with a business. I don't mean to get on a soap box but I'm really tired of the open season on profit. Sure, there are greedy bastards who do nothing but line their own pockets while their companies suffer but they're the minority. Most business owners are pouring their profit right back into their businesses to make the businesses stronger. Besides, without profit, we're out of business. It's a simple equation. Lean is a tool that increases profit. It's important to understand that increased profit is the end result of a company operating more efficiently and that's what Lean does for us. As an example, you wanted that new deburring machine. Remember?"

"Sure. Made my job a helluva lot easier. And faster."

"Right. That machine cost $ 15,000.00. Profit made that possible."

Ty didn't know what to say.

"Knowing you, Ty, it won't be long until you want another piece of equipment, especially when you're operating your own cell. You have a sharp eye and do a good job keeping abreast of technology."

"Thanks but that's part of my job."

"Yes and you do it well. The more efficient your cell operates, the more profit it will generate."

"And the sooner I can get a new piece of equipment, when I find one that we need," Ty said.

"Exactly and no doubt you'll want to upgrade, knowing you, Ty."

"You did mention my kids' college education," Ty said, pausing.

"Yes?" John asked.

"Frankly, I'm going to be expecting a raise. Doing all this Lean stuff is additional work."

Hearing the word 'raise', the employees who'd been listening to their conversation moved closer to them.

"Yes," Kurt said. "Let's talk about raises."

A muscle in John's jaw was clenching. He looked around at the group of employees and started to speak before really thinking his thoughts through when he felt a tug at his foot.

Prophet had grabbed the shoelaces of his right boot and was tugging at them. John lifted up his right foot which sent Prophet spiraling backward and he landed on his behind and yipped.

John knelt down and Prophet rushed back to him and began licking his hands as he re-tied his boot.

Re-tying his boot gave John a moment to collect his thoughts and he patted Prophet on the head before standing up and addressing the small group of employees.

"As we discussed during the employee meeting, compensation based on performance is part of the Lean process. Once the structure has been set, you'll have greater control over your own ability to earn money like you never have before."

"That's great, John, but in the meantime, how about a raise?" Kurt said.

"That's a very interesting point and maybe it's something we should discuss. ATMI is going Lean. There's no discussion on that. However, I had planned on holding off the compensation program until we had this Lean process up and running reliably. Now, if you'd like to bump up the compensation part of the program, we can discuss that."

Kurt looked at John and wasn't sure exactly what he was hearing.

"Well," Kurt said, "I would like to control how much I make."

"I understand that," John said. "After all, that's part of the philosophy of capitalism."

"Yeah," Kurt said. "That'd be great, being able to have control. That way, I wouldn't have to wait for the annual review."

"No, you wouldn't, if we put the compensation package in place now," he said. "Don't forget accountability, though."

"What's the catch?" Ty asked.

"There's no catch. But, you need to be aware of the situation before deciding if that's what you want to do now."

"Situation?" Ty asked, knitting his eyebrows together.

"Sure. It's a two-way street. We're undertaking a major change going to Lean. There are going to be mistakes and missteps along the way. You and everyone else are being asked to take on more responsibility. I was planning on introducing the new compensation package once we had it running smoothly. But, if most people are interested in going to that now..." his voice trailed off and he shrugged his shoulders.

Tuck had joined the rapidly growing group and slowly made his way up to John. He'd heard enough to be concerned. *"What in hell are you thinking, John?"* he wondered.

"Just how would this work?" Kurt asked.

"For starters, Aeroquip wants a three percent reduction in their new orders which we're starting next week. So, when we start that production, everyone involved will take a three percent reduction in wages."

"You mean I'm going to get less money?" Kurt said, his voice going squeaky with frustration.

"Well," John said, "I'm sure with the new Lean processes, you'll all be able to improve both quality and quantity. Therefore, less scrap, fewer rejections and higher production numbers. It should wash out."

"Wash out, hell," Kurt said. "I'm just learning about Lean. Now, don't get me wrong. I think Lean's a great idea but I'm not up to speed on it yet. I'll need a little time to get a handle on it."

"Okay," John said, "I understand that." He paused dramatically. "But, I don't think Aeroquip will say, "Okay, we'll take our three percent reduction when you get up to speed, Kurt. They're taking it now."

"Hey, it's not just me. Everyone has to learn."

"I know."

"I can't afford a three percent reduction. I can't afford a one percent reduction. I thought you said Lean was going to increase profitability."

"It is and it will, once we get it fully underway," John said.

"Besides, I'm running out of components and I don't control that," Kurt said.

"Kan-ban."

"Huh?"

"Kan-ban is the process where you notify others, through a card system which we will computerize, when you're running low on parts and someone will restock you."

"That sounds great but it's not running now."

"No," John said. "It's coming very soon, though. Any other problems?"

Kurt, feeling very much as if he was sitting on a stove that someone had turned on, paused.

"Yeah. My area's a mess. I hate to admit this but I spend too much time hunting for things. I'll be missing a wrench and will have to hunt for it. That slows my production down."

"5-S."

"What?"

"5-S is a system for organization. It stands for sort, set in order, shine, standardize, and sustain. We're going to be doing that shortly, too. That should take care of the disorganization."

"That's just dandy but until it's done, I'm going to be struggling with a three percent income reduction, right?"

"It looks that way if we bump up the compensation part of Lean."

"Oh, boy. Ty, you're the one that got us into this mess. Now get us out," Kurt said, laughing nervously.

"Me?" Ty said. "How's this my fault?"

"Pushing John for a raise." He looked around the manufacturing floor. "Look at this place. It's a mess. Parts and tools are everywhere. How long do you think it's going to take us to get it straightened up? To S-five it?"

"Five-S," John said.

"Hell, I don't know," Ty said. "You're talking alphabet and number soup to me and I don't fully understand what it means."

Faced with the bleak realities as John had laid them out, the employees who had gathered around began talking loudly among themselves. First, as a group, they'd perked up their ears with the thoughts of increased compensation and now, they were on the edge of becoming a mob, fighting over the loss of income.

Turk jammed his hands in his pockets. He saw the anger increasing in the employees' faces and didn't know what to do. In the meantime, John had knelt down and was playing with Prophet.

Ty was getting more nervous by the second.

"Hold up here," Ty finally said. "Let's back up. What if we just leave things the way they are?"

"Change is the only constant," John said. "We're going Lean and that's a whole passel of changes."

"No one told me I'd be taking a cut in pay!" someone shouted from the small group.

John stood up and looked at the group but no one admitted to the remark.

"I didn't want anybody to take a cut in pay," John said. "I know people are frustrated with all the changes about Lean and, so it seems, they're also tired of our compensation policy. I know Lean's going to make this company more profitable. I know that," he said with added emphasis.

No one else spoke.

"I was planning on keeping the same compensation package until we got Lean well underway so employees wouldn't have to worry about mistakes costing them income. ATMI can withstand the additional costs of Lean and I thought it would be better for the company to keep that burden. But, if people are eager to take that on as well…" His voice tapered off and he shrugged his shoulders.

"John, do you, in your heart of hearts, believe that Lean will increase productivity, quality and profit?" Kurt asked.

"Yes. In my heart of hearts, I do."

"And, you're willing to keep us at our same pay, with normal raises, the way it is now, until we get Lean underway? Once that happens, you'll bring out the new compensation package that gives us more control over our income?" Kurt said.

"That was my plan, Kurt. But, I've always prided myself on listening to the employees."

"Yeah, well, maybe you listen too damned much," Ty said and laughed.

"I don't like living on the corporate dole," Jock said, speaking for the first time since the group had gathered.

"Don't get me wrong but I don't want John doing me any favors. I want a fair wage for a fair day's work. If the company's taking hits, like this three percent reduction, we should all take the hit. I don't want to be beholden to anyone. No offense intended, John."

"None taken," John said.

"Shit and shinola!" Ty said. "You just signed our death warrants, Jock."

"No, he didn't," John said. "I wasn't doing anyone any favors by changing the compensation as the last piece of Lean. I thought, and still do, think it's the fairest thing. I'm the one who made the decision to go Lean. I know it's going to cost us to make this change. Why would I want to penalize the people who work here?"

"But, then, why even consider changing the compensation where we could make more money?" Kurt asked.

"Because I believe in capitalism. Because I believe in profit. I don't think it's a dirty word. I sincerely believe that ATMI is going to be more profitable with Lean. I also know it's going to require different skills from everyone who works here to make it successful. Just like a new hire. When we bring on a new employee, he's not making money for this company at first. He has a lot to learn and I pay for that. Or the company pays for it, I should say. I view this as the same thing. The only change is under the old system, the new employee would be entitled to the standard raises, as is everyone. It feels like my responsibility to keep pay stable through these changes. Under the new system, people have a chance to improve their income based on their performance."

"Works for me," Ty said.

"I'll go one better," Kurt said. "Now, you can call this selfish, but I'm going to do everything I can to get ATMI on-board with Lean as soon as possible. That just means more coins in my pocket."

"Fair enough," John said. "So, we'll keep pushing Lean and when it's in place, we'll address the new compensation package?"

"That's the ticket," Ty said.

"Okay," John said. "Then, let's get back to work…"

Kurt cut him off.

"Hold up a second. Who's going to be responsible for that 5S stuff you talked about?"

"How about you?"

"Sure. I'll take it on," Kurt said. "What about the other things…like that kanna-banana thing?"

"Kan-ban," John said, smiling.

"I'm overseeing that," Tuck said, "But, I'll need everyone's input. In fact, I'm putting together the plan for the first cell. Any volunteers?"

Both Kurt and Ty raised their hands.

"Okay, let's talk about that after lunch," Tuck said.

John slipped away from the group, tapping his leg to keep Prophet by his side. Tuck caught up with him as he reached his office.

"Well, Captain Bligh, you just about had a mutiny out there," Tuck said.

"I don't think so," John said. "Tuck, we've been running this place with a pretty tight fist. That type of management won't work with Lean. You, of all people, have complained about having to babysit employees."

"True."

"You and I are going to have to make some changes, too. Part of those changes is becoming comfortable with some very open and frank discussions. Remember, the employees are going to be calling the shots on quality in the very near future. If I'm going to respect a man enough to grant that, then, I better respect him enough to discuss and listen to his ideas on the money he's making."

Tuck sat down across from John and Prophet immediately began tackling one of Tuck's boots.

"Hey, pup, knock that off," Tuck said, gently pushing him away.

"That pup caused me to pause before opening my mouth. I think I'll call it a pause for profit. I was ready to strangle Ty until Prophet attacked my boot laces. Taking ten seconds to re-tie my boot, with no help from the pup, gave me the ten seconds I needed to keep my cool."

"How do you spell that 'pause'?"

"P A U S E," John said.

"Better make that P A W S," Tuck said. "Pun intended. Something else happened out there which is pretty damned neat. They're fired up about Lean now. They see that they have something to gain."

"Good point. Now, to keep the momentum rolling."

19

A week later, John was seated on the mezzanine of ATMI, overlooking the production floor. He was on his third pair of shoelaces, thanks to Prophet who was three feet from John's chair, trying to get the best of a rawhide bone.

John was feeling a fair sense of satisfaction. Lean was moving far faster than he'd expected.

"Estelle said I'd find you up here," Paul Conner said.

"Hey, glad you stopped by," John said, standing up and shaking hands with Paul. He grabbed a chair and put it beside his, motioning for Paul to sit down as he sat down again.

"They're moving like gangbusters down there," John said.

Paul looked over the railing and turned to John, his face stark.

"What in blazes is going on down there, John?" he asked.

"Lean. That's what. Kurt's taken over the 5-S and is only monitoring now. Ty's going to be launching the first cell, probably very shortly, and Tuck's teaching a group about kan-ban."

Once John had explained all the activity, Paul looked even more concerned.

"Have you taken complete leave of your senses?" Paul asked.

"You know, it takes a pretty gutsy man to stand in my building and tell me I've gone nuts."

"You have and I am."

Prophet had picked up the rawhide bone and trotted to John. He reached down and tossed the bone a few feet away, sending Prophet scurrying for it. When he retrieved the bone, he dropped it and began sniffing around Paul's shoes.

"Lucky you're wearing slip-ons. Otherwise, he'd have your shoelaces in tatters," John said.

"Cute pup," Paul said, reaching down and petting him.

Playing with the pup, and definitely not looking at John, Paul said, "I wonder if I can teach him to sit up, play dead, and roll over all at once."

"You'd confuse the hell out of..." John broke off his sentence.

"Hmmm...." Paul said. "You're probably right."

"Like hell you are!" Someone shouted from the manufacturing floor. The shout brought John to his feet.

Newton Nester, the tool crib manager, was standing guard at the chain-link doorway to the crib.

"There ain't no way in hell you're getting that multiple tool holder out of this tool crib to keep at your work station," he yelled.

Ty stood defiantly in front of Newton.

"That's what Lean is all about, Newton. I'm running my own cell which means I get my own tools. Period. Now, give me the damned tool holder."

"And, when every other yahoo in here wants a tool holder, I'll send them to you," Newton said. "See how you like that."

"No one's getting my tool holder from me. Once it's in my cell, it's staying there."

John observed the scene and was glad to see that Tuck was heading over to Newton and Ty. What he wasn't glad about was that ten employees who had been learning kan-ban from him were right on his heels. *But, what else were they supposed to do, now that their teacher had interrupted the training?* he thought.

Newton folded his arms over his chest, standing before the tool crib like a Viking warrior.

"What's the problem?" Tuck asked.

"This knucklehead wants me to give him a multiple tool holder to keep at his work station."

"Work cell," Ty interrupted.

"I only have three tool holders in the whole shop. I give one to Ty for his exclusive use, what am I supposed to do about everyone else?"

"I need the tool holder in my cell. You know I do, Tuck. I can't get production out on a timely basis without having that. Yet, the keeper of the castle won't let me have it."

"We'll buy one for each cell that needs one," Tuck said.

"Great," Ty said. "Now, give it to me, Newton."

"Oh, I'll give it to you all right. I ain't letting it go until I have enough for everyone. You think I want John jumping my case because some operator's screaming to high heaven that he couldn't get out production because he couldn't get a tool holder from me? Ain't gonna happen."

"Everybody, just settle down," Tuck said. "We'll get this sorted out."

John had heard enough and started toward the stairway.

"Hold up, John," Paul said. "You can't run interference every time there's a problem. Let them work it out."

"I'd prefer they work it out without any bloodshed," John said.

"Well, you're the one who turned them loose too fast," Paul said. "I don't know how you got them so fired up and enthusiastic. That's great. But, you're asking them to make changes far too fast."

"I got them fired up because of money. Good old profit."

Hearing his name, Prophet perked up his ears.

"Not you, boy. The dollars and cents kind of profit," John said.

"Paul," John said, continuing, "They're fired up to get Lean going as fast as they can so they can get to the compensation part of the program. I thought it was sheer genius to motivate them like that, although Tuck did call me Captain Bligh." He smiled. "In all honesty, it was this pup. Long story short, I was about to nail one of our employees because he was talking raises, and Prophet tackled my boot lace. Re-tying my boot gave me a few moments to consider my words more carefully. You'd said that change was difficult but if people are fired up about it, to me, that takes the greatest sting out of it. They're gung-ho."

"Uh-huh," Paul said. "Old habits die hard, not to use a cliché but it's true. You've yanked or well, maybe they've jumped out of their comfort zones. And, as my wife would say, the testosterone levels are running a mite high."

"What's your point?" John asked.

"Let me back up here a second. Did you say you were done with 5-S?"

"Yes."

"How'd that happen so fast?"

"I bought several 5-S kits from Don Tapping. They're great. The kit contains everything anyone would need to do 5-S. Kurt took it on and was done in two days flat. Now, we're all just monitoring."

"I think you're going too fast."

"Oh, this said by the person who told me his company wants a three percent cost reduction with the next order."

"John, you know we work with a lot of small to middle-sized job shops. Most of them are owned by an individual, not part of a corporate conglomerate. You know what the major complaint I hear from their employees is? It's that the owners are always getting on the band wagon of the latest idea."

"I don't get what you mean."

"The owner will read a book, like the One Minute Manager, think it's a great idea and buy copies for all of the employees and tell them to put it in place now. The following week, he'll walk in with a new book and the cycle starts over. The owner's always looking for the best ideas but often lacks consistency and follow-through."

"I'm not going to change my mind about Lean next week," John said.

"No, I don't think you will, but when your employees run into trouble, and I'll bet you a steak dinner at Sam's they will, you may be tempted to drop Lean."

"I'm committed, Paul."

"I believe that and your employees seem to be committed, but you've taken on a great deal in a very, very short period of time. That concerns me."

"You're really taking this 'helping out the supplier' seriously."

"That brings me to the real reason why I stopped over, and I'm doing this out of friendship, not as a customer. Just between us, how's it going with Frank?"

"He's very reluctant. I think I understand why. The whole cell concept, operator independent, has really threatened his power base. I have some grave concerns. Now, why do you ask? Between us as friends."

"I don't know that he's said anything negative about ATMI, other than he doesn't agree with the changes, but I do know he's looking for a job."

"That doesn't surprise me. I've been collecting resumes."

"Frank's well qualified and respected in the field. I don't think he'll be looking long. Your quality person is crucial to going Lean. You need to have someone who really understands the quality standards to help train the operators."

"I know Frank's having problems with this and I'm doing what I can to make this as peaceful as possible for him. If the quality shift from cop to coach works, I think he'll be okay."

"I see where you're going. The last thing you need right now is a brand-new head of quality."

"That may not be something I can avoid," John said. "If he's looking, I can't chain him here. Wouldn't even want to."

"Be creative. You may want to bring Frank's replacement on board to get trained by Frank."

"That would be a little obvious, wouldn't it? Frank's not dumb. He'd know instantly…"

"I'm not talking about keeping it from Frank. Tell him."

"I'd like to keep Frank, if at all possible. I was hoping the rapid transition to Lean would let him see that it's a good thing and he'd stay on."

"How likely is that?"

"I don't know. I'll have to think about that," John said.

"I'm flying out to one of our locations and want you to join me. It'd be good for you to benchmark a facility that has already gone Lean. Took them a few months, maybe even a year or two, though," Paul said, grinning. "There's also an ulterior motive. The quality manager wants to get back to Michigan. His wife is quite ill. If you like him, he might be a good fit here. I found out about it because his transfer request showed up on my desk. Selfishly, I'd rather have him working for you than a competitor."

"I'll go meet him but no promises. I owe Frank allegiance. If he can make the transition, I'd like to keep him and he's done nothing that warrants me blindsiding him."

"I understand and respect that," Paul said. Paul noticed that John was getting more fidgety by the second.

"It's hard for you to stand by, isn't it?" he asked. "Let's take a walk on the floor and see if we can ease some of your anxieties."

Both he and John headed for the stairwell with Prophet trotting at their heels.

"What's with the pup," Paul asked. "New mascot for ATMI?"

"Nah, I'm puppy sitting for a couple of weeks. Actually, he's pretty good company and I'm going to miss him when his family returns."

Once they'd reached the manufacturing floor, they walked up to the tool crib.

"How's it going?" John asked.

Newton was busy looking through a machining supply catalogue. Hearing John, he put the catalogue down.

"Getting ready to spend some of your money," Newton said. "It's going to cost a bundle."

"What are you talking about?" John asked.

"If every cell has to have every tool, it's going to cost. I'm just starting to compile the inventory."

"Not every cell has to have every tool," John said.

"That's not what they said," Newton answered.

"If cell A doesn't have a need for a carbide boring bar, they don't need to have one in their cell. However, if Cell A and Cell B both need high-speed steel boring bars, they'll each need one. So, before you can compile an inventory of what you want to buy, you're going to need an inventory of each cell's needs. Since we're doing this in stages, you're going to be ordering things one or two cells at a time. Not every cell all at once."

"I'm just doing what I'm told, boss," Newton answered.

"Tuck will let you know what parts need to be ordered," John said.

Leaving Newton to his catalogue, Paul and John walked over to the side where Tuck was conducting kan-ban training. They stood in back of the small group and watched as he went through a flip-chart presentation of the principles of kan-ban.

"Hey, John," Carter Alson said. "This stuff about street lamps is fascinating."

"Street lamps?" John asked.

"Not street lamps," Mike Marston said, good naturedly punching Carter in the shoulder. "Stop lights. That's the analogy. Green—go, yellow—slow, and red—whoa."

In an aside to John, Paul said, "I've never heard kan-ban discussed that way but it makes sense."

"Hell, yes," Carter said. "You have no idea how frustrating it is to run out of material and have to stop production. You can bet your bottom dollar that I'll be screaming to high heaven if my income is affected because I've run out of materials."

"Then, you have to know the rate at which you're using the materials," Mike said. "No one's a mind reader."

"Hell, before, I just ran the parts until I was out of stuff. Now, when I'm getting low, I'll start waving that red card like a bull fighter's cape and someone better get me what I need."

Tuck ended his presentation and sent everyone to lunch.

"How's it going?" John asked.

"It's going."

"That doesn't sound encouraging," Paul said.

"It's the flow that they seem to be missing. They can't give me any idea of their materials needs."

"How could they?" John asked. "They've never been held accountable for running their own cell. You just watch Ty. Once he has a handle on his cell, he'll be able to give you an accurate accounting. Without any data, it's unpredictable, but the data's there. We just haven't tracked it. Ty will be our guinea pig on that," John said.

"Good. He'll start his cell right after lunch."

Paul only shook his head while maintaining his silence.

"Are we moving too fast?" John asked of Tuck.

"I don't know," Tuck answered, scratching his head. "I guess I'm astonished at what the operators don't know. They're so used to doing their part of the job, until a drill bit breaks or whatever, shutting down their stations to get a replacement. No one can tell me how many drill bits they'll use up in six months. Keeping inventory on hand is going to be rough at first, but we'll get the hang of it."

"Don't count on keeping a high load of inventory," John said. "That's one of the first areas of cost reductions I expect with Lean."

"I don't see how inventory is going to be lowered until we're well underway," Tuck said. "There are just too many unknowns and we can't risk shutting production down because we're out of something."

"Think about it this way," Paul said. "How many ink pens are you going to use in the next three months?"

"Hell if I know," Tuck said. "I keep a couple on my desk and a couple in my shirt pocket. When one runs dry, I toss it and get another one."

"Is that how it happens?"

Tuck thought for a moment. "Yeah, pretty much."

"I don't think so," Paul said. "What I think really happens is what you've described is your intention. But, since you know your office supply cabinet is filled with them, you're not overly concerned if you lose one or if one runs dry. In fact, I bet you go to the supply cabinet when your last pen is out of ink or missing."

"Yeah, maybe."

"Okay. What if you only had one pen? What would you need to do differently to keep from not having a pen?"

Tuck puzzled for a moment, then said, "I'd have to know how much ink was in the pen, how long I could expect it to last, how much writing I'd be doing and how long it would take me to get a new pen."

"Right now," Paul said, "Those ink pens in your pocket are very replaceable, aren't they? Just go to the supply cabinet and grab a handful. But, as you just described, if you only had one pen, you'd know how much ink was in it, how long it would last, how much writing you'd be doing and how long it would take to get a new pen. Because, the last thing you'd want to happen would be to lose your pen or run out of ink. But, there's a lot of data you need to collect and know since that one pen has become so valuable to you."

As if to emphasize the point, Prophet dropped the rawhide bone he'd carried down from upstairs and put his right paw on it.

"Good dog," Paul said. "Think anyone's getting his one bone from him?"

Tuck laughed. "You're beginning to sound like my wife. She sent me to the store last night to get more milk. I told her I was dead-tired and would bring some home from work today. I also told her there still was some milk in the fridge. She said she'd be out of milk long before then, and I had to go to the store last night. Sure enough, we broke open that new bottle of milk during breakfast."

"Kan-ban was adopted from grocery stores, so your example is perfect. Grocery stores stock primarily perishables and have very small margins. So, they have to keep a sharp eye on how much milk to have on hand, the freshness dates, expected sales and when to re-order. That's kan-ban at work."

"You're telling me they knew that I'd be there last night at nine p.m.?" Tuck asked.

"Not you, in particular, but their data has shown them that X number of people will buy milk on any given day. They had milk when you went there, didn't they?"

"Got milk?" Tuck asked, laughing. "Sure, they had milk. How long did it take them to be able to anticipate the needs of their customers?"

"Probably quite a while, but in manufacturing, you don't have as many Tucks showing up at nine and wanting some extra machining as a grocery story has tired husbands showing up to buy milk at nine."

"Ty should be hearing this," Tuck said. "He has to get a handle on what his cell's going to be doing. That'll come from the production orders. He knows how his equipment operates and based on the orders and type of work, he should be able to anticipate drill bits, et cetera."

"The one thing he can't do is depend that the tool crib is going to have an abundance of his materials or tools. They need time to re-order. And, there's no sense in tying up literally hundreds of dollars in inventory."

"Hundreds?" John said. "Try thousands. Try hundreds of thousands of dollars tied up in inventory that's costing ATMI money every single minute."

"Yes," Paul said.

"I better get to work with Ty," Tuck said. "The kan-ban group will be back in half an hour but he should be involved in this now." He left John and Paul and headed toward Ty's work area.

"Okay," John said. "I'll go."

"Go?"

"With you. I'd like to see or, what'd you call it, bench mark a company that's gone through all of this. It has to be a day trip for me since I don't have anyone who can look after Prophet."

"No problem. The plant's in Indianapolis. We'll take the company plane. We'll fly out around six in the morning and be back before dark. How's Thursday for you?"

"Good. That's fine," John said.

"Great. I'll meet you at the private airport around 5:45 a.m. on Thursday."

Paul shook hands with John and left.

20

At 5:30 a.m., Thursday morning, John was finishing up his second cup of coffee, waiting for Paul in the lounge at Jackson's private airport. The sun had just risen and everything was bathed in a light sheen of gold. Dawn was one of John's favorite times. He watched a Citation taxi out to the runway and take off. He'd always wanted to learn to fly but never had the time.

He crumpled up his empty paper coffee cup, tossed it away and walked out of the lounge. A second plane was preparing for take-off. Unlike the Citation, the second plane was a Lear jet and mere seconds after leaving the runway, it streaked skyward, disappearing in the morning sun. The air was permeated with the smell of jet fuel.

John didn't hear Paul coming out of the lounge, due to the roar of the Lear jet and was a bit startled when he clapped him on the back.

"Morning, John," Paul said, extending his hand.

Standing next to John was a woman but he couldn't see her face. Due to the angle of the sun, she was backlit by the sunlight.

"John, I'd like you to meet Norma O'Malley."

John shook hands with her. Still blinded by the sun, he took a couple of steps to his right, causing her to take two steps to her left, which allowed John to get his first real look at her; she was about 5'4", trim and fit, with light auburn hair, sparkling hazel eyes and a brilliant smile. John thought she was gorgeous.

"Nice to meet you," John said. "I've always wanted to learn how to fly."

"It'll be good to have someone to talk to since Paul only sleeps on planes. I'm sure we'll find a moment or two to chat," she said, smiling.

John thought it was the most engaging smile he'd ever seen. Embarrassed, John realized he was still holding her hand and quickly released it.

"Ready to go?" Norma asked.

"Yes," Paul said and Norma left them.

"I'm not surprised she's distracted you and that's fine as long as you don't distract her. She's our pilot."

A few minutes later, a Beech King-Air taxied onto the tarmac and Paul headed toward it. John fell in step beside him.

Once aboard, Paul took a seat, secured his lap belt, and leaned back.

"Wake me just outside of Indy, please," he asked of no one in particular.

Norma was sitting in the captain's chair, making adjustments to the controls.

"Want to sit in the co-pilot's seat?" she asked John.

Without a moment's hesitation, John sat down in the co-pilot's seat, locked himself in the harness, looked at all of the instrumentation in front of him and took a deep breath.

"Here," Norma said, handing him a check list. "Sitting in that chair means work. Read off each item, one at a time."

John took the checklist and did as she asked. When Norma was satisfied that everything was good to go, she taxied the plane to the runway, spoke with the control tower, and pushed the throttle forward. The plane gained speed and lifted off the ground smoothly as it gradually won the battle against the earth's gravity.

The normal flight time to Indianapolis of an hour and a half seemed to take mere moments and the plane touched down at the Indianapolis airport. John was enthralled.

As Paul rousted himself from his light sleep, John thanked Norma for allowing him the first-hand experience of being in the cockpit.

"Thanks, Norma. It was really great. I've always wanted to fly and I think I'll seriously look into now. Your landing was as smooth as silk."

"Not bad for a woman driver, eh?" Norma said, grinning wickedly.

"Not bad for any driver," John said. "How will you spend your time while we're at X and L stamping?"

"Ohhh...." she looked around at the other planes at the private terminal, "Maybe a few drag races on the tarmac." John looked at her in surprise.

Seeing John's facial expression, she said, "Not to mention the pilot responsibilities, such as the Jeps charts, refueling, submitting the return flight plan, checking the air in the tires, and I'll probably grab a bite to eat." She grinned again.

"Well, I'll see you when we get back," John said.

"More importantly, you'll see me back in Jackson," Norma said.

Paul and John went to X and L Stamping and were greeted by Galvin Booth, the operations manager. He took them on a guided tour of X and L Stamping, giving John a first-hand view of Lean in action. The facility reminded him of a Swiss clock—individual units performing their functions in tight unison as part of the whole. He thought of the chaos going on at ATMI and knew going Lean was the best decision he could make. Galvin was more than open in discussing how they went Lean, bumps and all. Paul had tried to get John to benchmark other companies before but he'd never really seen the value in it until now. When he'd had all of his questions answered, Galvin offered to provide any additional assistance to him and ATMI if they needed or wanted it.

"Galvin," Paul said, "As usual, you've been great. Thanks for your time. We're going to wander down to Nate's office now."

"Thanks for coming by. You know how to get to Nate's office, of course," Galvin said. "God knows you've spent enough time there but…" he paused dramatically, "That was before we went Lean. Again, good to see you, Paul, and nice meeting you, John. Let me know if there's any thing I can do to help."

"Thanks," John said as he followed Paul down the hallway to Nate's office.

Seeing a man busy at his computer, Paul gently tapped on the door before stepping inside. The man looked up at his visitors and motioned them to come in and take seats.

After introductions, Nate said, "God, it's good to see you, Paul."

"Nice to see you, too, Nate," Paul said. "Now, I think I'll go find a cup of coffee and leave the two of you to talk."

After he'd left, Nate said, "Paul told me a little about ATMI and I'm pleased you'd take a few minutes to talk with me. Paul told you about my situation?"

"Paul said you were interested in coming back to Michigan."

"Not exactly. I am going back to Michigan, one way or the other. My wife was first diagnosed with cancer four years ago but has been cancer-free until last month. I was working at the Saline facility for X and L Stamping when she was originally diagnosed. Her doctors are at the University of Michigan hospital and that's where she wants to go for treatment. Unfortunately, X and L closed its Saline facility so…" his voice trailed off.

"I'm sorry. That must be a terrible ordeal for you, for your wife…for your entire family," John said, feeling awkward.

"It was, and is, but my priorities are straight. She feels most comfortable and confident at U of M and tackling cancer is a family mission for us. That's why I'm moving back to Michigan. Paul said you might have an opening." He handed John his resume.

"Might being the operative word," John said. "I'd like to keep our conversation confidential," glancing over Nate's resume.

"Of course."

"Our present Quality Director is having some difficulty adjusting to Lean," John said.

"I can understand that. I hated it at first. Now I love it."

"If he's able to make the transition, we would not have an opening, but if he can't make the transition…well, I'd definitely be in the market for a new Quality Director."

"How's your progress converting to Lean going?"

"Paul says we're going too fast," John said. "I don't know, though. I think we have a pretty good handle on things. We're moving fast but I'm not sure that's bad."

"It's a whole new mindset," Nate said. "And old habits die hard. You obviously know your people better than me, but for us, it was two steps forward, one step backward, two steps forward."

"What was the hardest part?" John asked.

"Getting people to understand costs. I swear, I wanted to send all of them back to Econ 101."

John suddenly became much more interested in Nate Lunt. He was clearly speaking his language.

"Funny you should say that. Everyone's always teased me because I always counted my money every Sunday. It was a ritual for me, but I get extremely nervous if I don't know exactly where I am financially."

"Yeah. You get into some of the gray areas and, without a sharp eye, you're up to your hindquarters in alligators. But, for you, I think you're going to be pleasantly surprised by what Lean can do for your bottom line. My bet is you're going to discover a ton of hidden costs you didn't know were draining your company."

"You mentioned a change in mindset, Nate, and that's so true. For years, we were a time and materials shop. Not much need to worry about costs then. They were just billed to the customers."

"The good, ole days, eh?" Nate smiled.

"Yes. The good, ole days. But, as we both know, the only constant is change. Speaking of change, I can't make any promises about a position at ATMI, but I will take a thorough look at your resume and reference check, if you don't mind."

"Not at all. Everyone at X & L knows I'm leaving. Paul has said good things about you and your company. I'd like to discuss working for you in more detail if the opportunity arises."

As Nate was speaking, Paul knocked on the door, and said, "I don't mean to interrupt but we have a plane to catch."

After shaking hands with Nate, John and Paul headed back to the airport. As on the earlier flight, John sat in the co-pilot's seat, read the check list off to Norma, and watched intently as she expertly flew the plane back to Jackson.

When they'd disembarked, Norma said, "It was a pleasure meeting you. Thanks for the help."

"Now, wait a minute," John said. "You said I'd be seeing you in Jackson."

"We are in Jackson," she said, somewhat confused.

"I was thinking more along the lines of dinner," John said.

"Oh. Uhhh…that'd be nice," she answered.

"Great. How's tonight?"

"A little quick but…okay."

"I have to stop at home first to take care of a dog I'm watching, so shall we meet at Gilbert's? Say around seven o'clock?"

"That sounds fine."

21

John arrived at ATMI mid-morning. He was running low on puppy food and had to stop at the pet store with Prophet in tow. Unfortunately, he didn't have a leash and within two minutes, Prophet managed to knock over a carousel of canned dog food, terrorize a Siamese cat who was minding his own business, and throw himself into the bin of rawhide bones.

After rounding up Prophet and getting what he needed to the checkout stand, John gave the clerk an extra twenty dollar bill for Prophet's mess. The clerk tried to refuse but John insisted she take the extra money. As a token of her appreciation, she gave John a red rubber ball for Prophet, much to the pup's delight.

John went to his office and gave Prophet the rubber ball and a rawhide bone to distract him from any more mischief.

Tuck walked in and without any preamble, said, "We have a problem."

"What?"

"We shipped an order to Carrywise that didn't meet specs."

"How'd it happen?"

"Ty was running the cell and doing a fine job of it, and...and I thought everything was okay. He shipped the parts but Carrywise rejected the entire lot. With good reason, I might add. There was a change in their specs. They'd faxed it over yesterday but Ty didn't know about it. He said he asked Frank to take a look at the parts but Frank said he was sure they were okay. Turns out they weren't."

"Did Frank tell Ty about the new specs?" John asked.

"I don't know. I was just on his way to his office when you showed up. Thought I'd talk with you first."

"What are you doing about Carrywise?"

"We're remachining the parts. It's the only thing we can do. I explained to them about Lean and they seemed understanding but I don't want to screw up with them again. So, I'll be checking these parts before they go out."

"You go work with Ty and I'll talk with Frank," John said. They both left John's office and headed in separate ways.

As John walked into Frank's office, Frank was on the telephone. John heard him say, "The opportunity sounds good—." Frank saw John and then, quickly added, "I'll have to call you back."

"How was your trip?" Frank asked as he hung up the telephone receiver.

"Learned a great deal. It's amazing what Lean can do for an organization. What can you tell me about the Carrywise situation?"

"I guess we shipped them non-conforming parts."

"Guess?"

"No. Not guess. That's what happened."

"How'd it happen?"

"I'm kind of out of the loop on it, John," he said.

"Tuck said Carrywise told him they'd faxed over new specs. He also told me that Ty asked for your sign-off on the parts and you said they were okay."

"What I told Ty was I was sure he knew what Carrywise expected."

"What made you so sure?"

"I trained him on the specs," Frank answered.

"On the old specs? What about the new ones? Did you make sure Ty knew about those?"

"John, isn't a cell supposed to be self-contained? How did I know Ty didn't get a copy of the fax?"

"How did you know he did get a copy?"

"I didn't, but I'm an awfully high-priced errand boy if all I'm supposed to do is run around making sure everyone gets any faxes I got. I guess you think the Carrywise problem is my fault."

"I'm not interested in fault. I'm interested in correction and elimination of future occurrences. Tuck is working with Ty to handle the correction. They're remachining the parts. As far as elimination, this has brought up a hole we didn't think about. Customers need to communicate directly with who's responsible. That'll be an educational process. We probably need to be looking into computer links between cells and customers."

John paused waiting for any reply from Frank. None was forthcoming.

"Frank, until we come up with something better, it is your responsibility to make sure everyone in this place is acquainted with all of our customers' specifications."

"Who's got the time…"

"You do. As I said, we need to find an alternative but until we do, it's yours. You'll have plenty of contact time while you're training the quality classes."

"You expect me to still do all the quality training, stay in touch with the customers and make sure everyone else knows what the customer wants?" His incredulity was clearly written on his face.

"Yes."

Not giving Frank a chance to answer, John turned on his heel and strode away. He was furious beyond belief and it took a great deal of restraint not to fire Frank on the spot. Nate Lund was looking better all the time.

Still chewing on his anger, he went to Ty's cell. Both Tuck and Ty were busily remachining the Carrywise parts. The cell looked like a tornado had struck.

"We're just about done, boss," Tuck said. "Only five more parts and they'll be ready to ship."

John held his tongue and watched as patiently as he could until the last five parts were finished.

"Tuck, make sure you ship those priority and also send a fruit basket. We blew it with Carrywise and anything we can do to build goodwill certainly won't hurt."

"Good idea," Tuck said, bundling up the last parts. When he was finished, he left Ty's work cell.

"Ty, when are you going to implement 5-S in this area? That should've been done before you went operator-independent."

"It has been implemented," Ty said.

"In whose mind?" John asked.

"Tuck worked on it with me," Ty said, somewhat defensively.

"Your work cell looks like a fourteen angry monkeys had a brawl."

"Everything I need is here!" Ty said.

"5-S means having everything you need when you need it where you need it," John said.

"Then, I'm home free, Ty said."

"Okay. Let's do a little experiment. First, close your eyes."

"Huh?"

"That's right. Close your eyes," John said. "And, no peeking."

Ty reluctantly closed his eyes.

"Now, pick up internal micrometer," John said.

Ty hesitated at first, then, began fumbling around like a child playing Pin the Tail on the Donkey. After a few seconds, Ty gave up, opened his eyes, hunted a bit longer and finally grabbed the mic.

"Remember your dad's work bench in the garage?" John asked.

"Yeah. He had a pegboard with all of his tools hanging on it. He even had tape outlining where each tool belonged. He went apeshit if someone didn't return a tool."

"That's a big part of 5-S and you're not there yet. Before you start on the next order, 5-S your area completely, including the tape outlines," John said. "Then, keep your work cell looking like that."

"You're serious, aren't you?"

"As a State Trooper when you're going fifteen over the limit."

Leaving Ty to his 5-S activity, John returned to his office.

When he walked into his office, all he saw of Prophet was the pup's rump sticking out from under the credenza. Hearing John, Prophet wriggled out from the credenza and greeted him as only a pup can.

John sat down at his desk, heavy-hearted. They had gone too fast in their transformation to Lean. Hearing a *thunk*, John looked back at his credenza and saw that Prophet was trying his best to get under it. He got down on his knees to see what was enticing the pup. Against the wall, he saw the red rubber ball. He reached for it and gave it to Prophet. The pup chewed on it for a few seconds, dropped it and picked up his rawhide bone. In the meantime, the ball rolled back under the credenza. Seeming to notice that the ball was gone again, Prophet thunked his head one more time, trying vainly to get under the credenza.

John picked up the rawhide bone and tried to distract the pup but he wouldn't be dissuaded. It was clear he wanted both the ball and rawhide bone simultaneously.

"Listen, if you think I'm going to spend my day retrieving your ball, you're nuts," he said to the dog who paid him no mind at all and kept trying to dig his way under the credenza.

Concerned that Prophet would eventually start tearing up the carpeting, John once again retrieved the rubber ball and tossed it across his office. Prophet tore after the ball, grabbed it and trotted back to John's desk. He dropped the ball and picked up the rawhide bone.

"Why don't you make up your mind?" he asked the pup.

"Why don't I make up my mind? Why doesn't Frank make up his mind?" he thought. Why not, indeed.

John stood up and went to the doorway of his office.

"Estelle, hold my calls and I don't want to be disturbed," he said, closing the door to his office. After returning to his desk, he got out Nate Lund's resume and began calling references. All of Nate's references checked out magnificently.

Then, he called Nate. After discussing the financial terms of a possible employment offer, he asked Nate when he could start.

"John, as I mentioned, my family is my first priority and I'm leaving X and Y as soon as possible. They know that and my replacement has already started."

"How long do you think it'd take you to get up to speed at ATMI?"

"Candidly, I've discussed ATMI with Paul and he's briefed me as much as he could. You have two major product lines and both of those product lines are very similar to X and L. I don't want to overstate my abilities but I think I could be up to speed in sixty days."

"That would include training our employees on Lean, you know."

"Yes."

"If sixty days is the ideal, what would be the minimum time you'd need?"

"Paul said you were not one to hesitate. If push came to shove, I'd have a reasonable confidence level after thirty days."

"If I make an offer, when could you start?"

"Would next Monday be too soon?" Nate asked.

"Not at all. I'll get back to you. Thanks for your time and I'll be in touch within a day," John said, terminating the telephone call.

Now for the tricky part. He mentally prepared how he'd approach Frank as he walked toward Frank's office. As before, he interrupted Frank in a telephone call that Frank rapidly terminated.

John walked in, closed the door to Frank's office and sat down.

"Frank, we've always been straight with one another and I don't see any reason for that to change now. Lean isn't for everyone. Based on what you've said and my observations, this transition isn't one you want to make."

"I told you I'd do my job," Frank said.

"That's the core of the problem. I'm redefining what your job is and it doesn't seem to be a comfortable fit for you."

"You said we'd always been straight so get straight to the point," Frank said. "Are you firing me?"

"No. Now, be as straight with me. Are you looking for another job?"

Frank's cheeks reddened slightly.

"I always keep an eye on what's available, John. That's only smart," he answered.

"Being straight, remember?"

"Well...ummm.... I'd heard about something at..." He couldn't look John in the eye.

"Let me make you a proposition. It's clear that you don't have the same belief in Lean that I do. You hold a critical position at ATMI. I need someone as the Quality Manager who is as committed to Lean as I am. I think we've come to a parting of the ways."

"So, you are firing me," Frank said.

"No. If I thought you were committed to Lean, we wouldn't even be having this discussion. I may have a win-win for you and ATMI. I'd like to offer you a three-month guaranteed severance package but I want the next thirty days devoted to ATMI and your primary responsibility would be to train your replacement. You would also be free to look for another job as long as it didn't interfere with ATMI. That's for the next thirty days. After that, you can divide your time between here and job hunting up to ninety days. Once you've found something, you could start immediately. That is, after the first month. Your severance package would kick in on the day of your departure. I'll give you excellent references."

"I'll have to think about it," Frank said.

"No. I need your answer now." John knew he was gambling but felt he'd moved fast enough that Frank didn't have another position already lined up and he knew, beyond a shadow of a doubt, that Frank wouldn't walk without someplace to go.

"What if I say 'No'?" Frank asked.

"You're an honorable man and we've had five good years working together. I will also believe that you're committed to the good of this company. I would expect no less from you as we adopt Lean and that I can depend on you to be here for the long haul."

Frank cleared his throat.

"It's a deal," he finally said.

"Okay. I'm sorry to lose you. I think you have a lot to offer any company and you've made significant contributions to ATMI. You will be missed." John stood up and extended his hand.

Frank shook hands with John and said, "You know, it just never would've worked out with me and Lean. It goes against my thirty years in quality. Funny, now that we've resolved this, I can feel the stress draining from me. Thank you for your understanding, John."

"I just want what's best for everyone."

"No, I mean it. You're being great to me and I…"

Now it was John's turn for his cheeks to redden and he became self-conscious with Frank's praise.

"Hey, there's a lot we have to do. I'll see you later," John said and left Frank's office.

When he was back in his office, he called Nate.

"Pack your bags. You start Monday," John said. "Frank Cazzlone is our present quality manager and I have a solid commitment for thirty days to get you up to speed. It may be a little longer, but Frank won't have to look too hard for employment so be prepared to hit the ground running when you get here."

As the day ended, Tuck sat down in John's office and said, "We'll be fine at Carrywise. They also liked the fruit basket. Nice touch."

"Good," John said.

"We're going to have to address this issue with Frank. I don't mean to crucify someone without a trial but..."

"It's been taken care of," John said,

"How so?"

"I've hired Nate Lund from X and L Stamping to take over quality. He'll be here on Monday. Frank knows this and has agreed to be here at least thirty days up to ninety to help Nate get up to speed."

"Good. I'll clear time Monday to interview...Nate. That's his name, right? I hate to see Frank go. Maybe we can change his mind."

"No. And an interview won't be necessary. I've already hired Nate. He's replacing Frank and will be starting Monday."

"Nate hasn't been interviewed by me or anyone else on the management team," Tuck said in a tone of voice almost as if reminding a school child he needed a note from his mother. "We all have to interview..."

"It's a done deal."

"John, with our emphasis toward team work and Lean, you can't just go out and hire someone."

"Whenever possible, I prefer the team approach but, as I said, whenever possible. This wasn't one of those times."

"That's not how we do things here, especially since we're going Lean," Tuck said, becoming petulant.

"Tuck, I agree with you completely, but Nate Lund was coming back to Michigan, one way or the other, as soon as he could. I had to move quickly. I would much prefer that everyone on the management team have a chance to interview him, but there simply wasn't time. You'll have to trust my judgment on this one."

"The team has to have final say," Tuck said but never got to add more before John cut him off.

"Whatever gave you the idea that going Lean meant that this company was going to be a democracy?"

22

Later that evening, John and Norma were finishing up the Chinese dinner she'd brought over. John had called her to cancel their second dinner date, explaining that he wasn't in a fit temper for man or beast and his back hurt. She suggested that she bring over Chinese and he'd reluctantly agreed.

After they'd cleaned up the dinner plates and stashed the left-overs in their white carry-out boxes in the refrigerator, John poured them both more wine and they went into his living room where he eased himself into his recliner.

"This was nice of you," John said. "It's been a hectic time and it's nice to kick back a bit."

"You do look pretty frazzled," Norma said.

"It's just everything that's going on at the company. We've needed to radically change the way we're doing business and we're doing it but it's taking its toll."

"Tell me about it," she said.

"Do you understand the concept of Lean manufacturing?" he asked.

"Somewhat, from what I've heard from Paul and what you said during dinner," she answered.

"The real key in Lean is to eliminate waste, like excess inventory, unnecessary movements, double checking things that should be done right the first time. It's a little hard to explain."

"It sounds like flying, Norma said.

"How so?"

"Every time I go up in a plane, a series of steps had to be taken to get that plane ready to go. I'm not a mechanic but I know our hangar is extremely efficient. Once I'm in the plane, everything better be ready. Then, it's my turn to do it right. When I first started flying, I wanted to carry a parachute…just in case," she said, laughing. "In fact, the first time I went for a distance flight with my instructor, I did take a parachute. He caught a glimpse of them as I was taxiing the plane for take-off. He made me stop and threw out the parachutes on the runway and then said, "Now go."

"I was shaking like an October leaf but he barked at me and so I took off. Once we were airborne, he said, 'Up here, you don't have time for 'Oops.' Do it right or don't do it."

"Sounds like a tough instructor," John said.

"He was the best and my second. I fired my first."

"Why?"

"Because he kept moaning about women flying, kept saying he didn't think it was such a good idea and certainly not as a commercial pilot. He actually had the audacity to ask me if I thought I could keep my mind on flying when I should be thinking about fixing dinner for my husband and kids. He's lucky I didn't toss him on the runway," she said.

"Tough lady," John said.

"I've been told that before but it's really disciplined passion."

"Disciplined passion?" John said quizzically.

"Yes. Lots of people want things but don't have whatever it takes to do it or they really feel safe doing what they've always done and want the change to happen magically. Disciplined passion is what it takes in my opinion to get something done. I was passionate about flying ever since I was nine years old but that passion alone wasn't enough. It had to be channeled into a constructive method, through discipline, to accomplish my goals. That's disciplined passion."

Prophet walked into the living room and sat down at the base of John's recliner. He looked up at him with his big puppy eyes and whined.

"Okay, boy," John said, starting to get up. "He needs to go for his evening walk."

"Here, I'll take him," Norma said.

"No, that's all right."

"Oh, for pete's sake, just sit there and relax. Where's his leash?" she asked.

"Hanging on the hook by the door," John said.

She stood up and went to the door, with Prophet right at her heels. John listened as she chatted with the puppy while attaching his leash. When he heard the back door close, he began mulling over her words about disciplined passion. Maybe that was what was lacking. Not all of the time but…enough that it was causing him discomfort. As she'd said, there's no time for 'Oops,' and he felt the same way about his business. No time for 'Oops.'

The next morning, John called Tuck and a few other managers into his office.

"Your priority right now is to get rid of every piece of excess inventory in this building. A hauler will be here at three to pick it up."

"Huh?" Tuck said.

"It's something called disciplined passion. We don't have time for 'Oops.' And, I believe that people are too dependent on grabbing another piece of metal if they make a mistake as well as being too dependent on others catching their mistakes. That's not the way a Lean operation works."

After getting his ears pinned back yesterday, Tuck wasn't about to question his boss, especially in front of anybody else so he said, "Cortez."

John caught the reference immediately although no one else did.

"Exactly, Tuck. Now explain it to the others."

All eyes turned to Tuck.

"When Cortez was conquering Mexico, it was going to be very rough which Cortez knew. Rather than have his men think longingly about their ships waiting as safe passage home, he burned all his ships. He only wanted his men thinking forward. That's what John's doing."

"I'm deadly serious about this, everyone," John said. "Do not hold back a single piece of excess inventory. You know what you need and that's all we're going to keep. Please don't let me catch you or anybody else stockpiling anything that's excess."

Danny Carlisle, an operator, said "You sound like my mother. We were really poor growing up. I mean really poor. When she'd cook dinner, she'd ask us how hungry we were and we had to be really honest with her. I don't know which was worse. Telling her we were more hungry than we were so food was left over or not telling her if we were really hungry. Did that a couple of times and went to bed hungry. Once my dad got a great job and we had good money coming in, I was fixing hamburgers on the grill. I fixed far more hamburgers than we could eat and she threw a fit. Said that just because we could afford it, that was no reason to waste money."

"That's it exactly. Those are both good examples. I don't want anyone thinking longingly of the good, old days or wasting money simply because we could afford it. If we continue to waste money, we'll run out. Now, get busy," John said.

Four hours later, as John was supervising the removal of all excess materials from ATMI, Nate Lund walked up to him.

"This is a pleasant surprise," John said.

"Hope you don't mind my starting early."

"Not at all, but aren't you busy? Finding a new house? Moving your family?"

"No, not really. When we moved to Indianapolis, we never sold the house, just rented it out. The tenants have agreed to let us break their lease and they'll be out in the next couple of weeks so I'll be staying at the Holiday Inn until they've moved. My wife is already packing."

"Is she…okay, I mean…" John's voice trailed off.

"Oh, yes. In fact, my coming up here early was her idea. She's felt pretty awful, psychologically, I mean, when the cancer came back. I think she felt useless. So, getting everything ready for the move is a great way to get her mind off it. On the other hand, maybe she just wanted to get me out of the house." He laughed.

"You two must have a really great marriage."

"It's a true partnership. What's going on here?" Nate asked.

"Tuck says I'm playing Cortez," John said and smiled. "Actually, a lady I met mentioned the phrase 'disciplined passion' and it made a lot of sense to me. I'm committed to Lean and everyone else is, or so they say. However, I suspect they're hedging their bets so I'm getting rid of every piece of excess inventory."

"Selling it?"

"Nope. Didn't want to take the time to find a possible buyer. I'm just trashing it."

"Oh," Nate said, raising his eyebrows. "Are you always this impulsive?"

"Impulsive has nothing to do with it. Committed. Like Tuck said, burning the boats. We're not looking back."

At that moment, Prophet came flying around the growing pile of scrap metal, his ears flying like brown flags, and a work boot in his mouth. He slid to a stop at John's feet, dropped the boot and put a paw on it.

"HEY!" Tuck yelled.

John and Nate turned to see Tuck hobbling after Prophet, minus one boot.

"Pup, that's MY boot, not yours," he said, as he squatted down next to the pup. Tuck started to pick up the boot and Prophet grabbed the laces, growling. They played a mock game of tug-of-war until Prophet finally released the boot.

"Nate, I'd like you to meet Randy Tucker, the Manager of Operations."

Tuck, staggering on one foot, while putting his boot on the other one, smiled sheepishly.

"Hi. Call me Tuck," he said, dusting off his hands and extending his right hand to Nate.

"And, this is Prophet," John said.

"Company mascot?" Nate asked.

"No. He belongs to a neighborhood kid and I'm puppy sitting while they're on vacation."

"When is Jimmy coming back?" Tuck asked. "That's the third time he's stolen my boot."

"Maybe if you'd keep them on your feet?" John suggested.

"Yeah, yeah, I know. But, they're new and I'm breaking them in. Oh, hell, why am I talking to you about my boots?" Tuck asked.

"Good point. How's this going?" John asked, motioning to the growing pile of scrap.

"Like pulling teeth. I'm having to check each station to make sure they're not holding back anything. Everywhere I go, I find they're keeping extras…'just in case' they keep saying. I have to admit that this is a good idea, John," Tuck said. "I'm having a rough time with Rick. All his big talk about becoming the best at Lean. I've found more material stashed in his area than anyone else and I keep finding more. He even had stuff in his toolbox. I hate a hypocrite."

"Speaking of the devil," John said as Rick emerged from the building, carrying a bin of material for the scrap heap.

Rick didn't see them standing there and as Prophet bounded up to him, Rick gave him a sharp kick in the ribs. "Get out of the way, you damned dog," he growled.

Prophet yelped in pain.

"Rick, that was cowardly," John said, kneeling beside Prophet, checking whether he was seriously hurt. Prophet sat up, shook his head and began licking his side. He wasn't seriously hurt but more scared. John petted him to reassure him.

"Rick, you're fired," John said. "Don't you ever think you can kick a dog in front of me and get away with it."

"What the…" Rick instantly broke off his words, seeing the look on John's face.

"Put that on the scrap pile and come with me. I'll get your final check cut immediately," John said.

Rick threw the bin with all the material in it on the scrap heap, muttering under his breath, then, walked with John into the building.

Prophet, torn between following his hero but avoiding his abuser, whined.

Tuck squatted down and called Prophet to him.

"You stay with me, boy," he said, petting the pup.

"Quite a day so far," Nate said.

"Welcome to ATMI," Tuck said.

Nate picked up a piece of rebar, examined it and tossed it back on the scrap head.

"I don't mean to give you the wrong idea about John. He's not some hot-headed lunatic."

"I didn't think that at all. I think he's a man who is very precise."

"Precise?" Tuck asked. "I'm not sure I know what you mean."

"How much money do you have in your billfold?"

"Huh?"

Nate laughed and asked again.

"How much money do you have in your billfold?"

"I guess forty or fifty dollars. Why?"

"I'll bet you lunch that John knows exactly how much money he has in his billfold." Nate stopped speaking as if that explained everything.

Tuck scratched his head and said, "Okay. I give up. What do you mean?"

"About being precise? Companies get in trouble all the time by being sloppy. Sloppy with their quality and productivity. Sloppy with their employees. Just sloppy.

I'm sure you've seen the picture of the boat floating in the water. The before and after picture? Before Lean, all the treacherous rocks are hidden beneath the water and the boat is in jeopardy just like the Titanic. After Lean, the rocks are visible and the boat stays safe. It's all about precision. Seeing what's in the water and not just the tips of the icebergs either."

"Didn't all the water help keep the boat safe, instead of putting at the level of the rocks?" Tuck asked.

"False sense of security. The rocks were still there and all the boat could see were just the tips, not the full depth of the rocks or the problems. I certainly don't know John well but it's my guess that the precision of Lean is one of the major factors that appealed to him."

"I see what you mean but John's not a tight-wad, either."

"Oh, heavens no. Didn't mean to imply that. The money in the billfold is just an example. If I'm right, and John does know exactly how much, it just shows precision. He needs to know where everything is in order to make informed decisions. I sure hope I'm right because it's the same philosophy I hold dear about quality. Everybody in this plant will know exactly what our quality standards are, if I have anything to say about it."

"Isn't that what you're here to do?"

"I certainly hope so and have every reason to believe so. But a lot of quality people give lip service and never really train or coach employees on the standards. They're always running around like little demi-gods, giving or rejecting as the mood strikes them. I hate that."

Tuck thought of all of the frustration the operators had felt through the years because of exactly what Nate had just described.

"That's music to my ears but, in defense of quality, they'll say that a customer changed the standard, that they're pushed for parts and will take everything or they're slow and won't take anything."

"That does happen but when a customer changes a standard, as soon as I know about it, so will everyone else. No secrets."

"Sounds good."

"And on that point, if a customer has tolerances of 1/1000, we'll work against tolerances of .05/1000 or a shade better than the customer has requested. We'll set our quality standards, higher than the customer."

"That's a radical approach."

"I know but it works. It's the way we drive our cars. There are lines on the road and we drive within those lines, right?"

"Yes."

"And, if the car starts to veer toward the line, you correct. That's what all of the quality tools are designed to do, to help people stay within the lines by letting them know when they're beginning to veer toward a line."

"You make it sound simple."

"It does sound simple and it is, in philosophy. The beauty is that it gets simple when everyone's taking the same approach. That's what Lean does. I know about Lean but have a great deal to learn about ATMI."

"I think you'll catch on pretty quickly, and I'll do everything I can."

As Tuck was telling Nate about ATMI, John approached them.

"John, how much money do you have in your billfold?" Tuck asked.

John cocked his head to the side and said, "Two hundred and seventy-three dollars. Why?"

"Oh, nothing. I'm just buying our new Quality Director lunch," Tuck said, slapping Nate on the back.

23

At the end of the week, three cells were up and functioning, shipping excellent parts to the customers. A fourth cell was starting and struggling, like a new-born foal, wobbly, fighting to stand up then run. Employees were rapidly turning to Nate with questions, having found him to be helpful in coaching them on quality standards. Good to his word, Frank was graciously turning the reins of quality over to Nate and providing him with every bit of assistance he could.

As the afternoon wore on, the second shift employees began arriving early and gathering on the outside patio. They were still buzzing about John throwing away over a million dollars' worth of inventory.

Tuck found Nate helping the fourth cell and said, "Come on. It's pizza time."

"Oh, thanks but I'll grab something to eat later," he said.

"Nah. It's sort of a tradition around here on the last Friday of the month. We all have pizza. Come on."

"Okay," Nate said, picking up a rag and wiping his hands.

They walked from the manufacturing floor, out through the side door to the patio. Nate had just taken a cold soft drink out of a tub of ice when John walked through the door, carrying a stack of pizzas.

"There's more to be brought in," John said, as he sat the pizzas down on the picnic table.

"That's something you won't see at a large corporation," Nate said to John. "The CEO delivering pizzas."

"It's not something you'd normally see here either, except I was at the door when the pizza guy arrived," John said smiling.

"You know what I mean," Nate said. "This whole 'Let's have pizza together' gets lost in the big companies."

"Yes, and that's something I'd hate to see lost here, but we are growing. Come on, grab some pizza and relax. It's been a busy week," John said.

Prophet, sure that all of the wonderful smells meant something good to eat, sniffed the air repeatedly. Knowing Tuck to be a soft touch, Prophet followed him as he sat down at the picnic table and was rewarded with a piece of pepperoni.

"John, I hate to admit it, but I'll miss the pup when he goes home but I will get to eat all of my lunch," Tuck said.

"His family should be home today so this is his last day here. I'm going to miss him, too," John said.

Ron Stabler, first shift foreman, sat down with John, Tuck and Nate, and also gave Prophet a piece of sausage from his pizza.

"I'm going to miss the little guy, too," Ron said. "But, I'm not going to miss all of these changes. I'm glad they're almost over."

"What's almost over?" Tuck questioned.

"Oh, you know, all the Lean stuff. We're just about done with 5S and we'll have the rest of the cells up by next week, then we can get back to business," Ron said.

Nate glanced at John and caught his eye.

"Ron, we're just getting started," John said.

"Started?" Ron said, spewing Coke out his nose. Coughing, he said, "I shouldn't talk and drink at the same time."

"Just getting started," John reiterated.

"You've turned this place upside down, thrown away over a million dollars' worth of inventory, reorganized the work into cells, and we're not done? We're going to keep living in this chaos?" Ron asked, genuinely surprised.

"These are permanent changes and we're going to keep making them," John said.

"That's an oxymoron," Tuck said.

"Lean isn't a bunch of changes we've made to fix the business. It's a process we're adopting to continually improve ATMI. Nate, help me out," John said.

"Ron, it's like a diet," Nate said. "If someone needs to lose weight and goes on a fad diet, they'll just regain the weight. But, if someone needs to lose weight and starts eating properly, they'll lose the weight more slowly but it'll stay off."

"We haven't done anything slowly," Ron said.

"No, and like Friday afternoon pizza, the rapid changes are part of being a small business. The advantage is to be to able change on a dime. The difficulty is to maintain the changes. That'll be the test for ATMI."

"I guess I'm still lost," Ron said.

"Lean isn't a change, like a new piece of equipment. It's a philosophy. John has elected to take ATMI to a Lean philosophy which means that everything will be under review on an on-going basis. There is no 'going back to the good, ole days.'"

"I am never going to tie up cash in excess inventory again," John said emphatically. "I am never and I mean never going to root through excess parts to complete a customer's order or to do a favor. Last time I did that it cost me $225.00. We're never going to agree to make parts that aren't part of our core competencies."

"But, that doesn't mean our core competencies can't change," Tuck said.

"Exactly," Nate answered. "We may find that we'll add core competencies or even drop some, depending on our expertise and our customer demands."

"Now, wait a minute," Ron interjected. "We're the best at shaping metal in the business. We're not giving that up, are we?"

"Good point," Nate said. "Now expand your thinking. Think of all the saddle makers when Henry Ford began mass-producing cars. Those that kept thinking of themselves as saddle makers went out of business. Those that realized their skill was in leather crafting began making boots, jackets and even car seats. They're the ones who survived."

"I think I'm beginning to see," Ron said.

"They kept refining their processes and examining new markets," Nate said. "Until they became fat, dumb and happy but, most importantly, forgot about their customers."

Ron took a bite of his pizza, mulling over Nate's words. "Yeah, like the phone company. My son wants a phone for his birthday. The one he wants is no bigger than a playing card and takes pictures. When I grew up, phones were the black desk models."

"That's what competition is all about," Tuck said. "And Lean is our best defense in maintaining a competitive edge."

"It's not a defense, it's an offensive strategy," Ron said. "Lean allows ATMI to be so sure of its' quality and productive capabilities that we'll know exactly what we can do and at what cost."

"It comes down to disciplined passion," John said. "You mentioned surviving a few moments ago. I'm not interested in surviving. I'm interested in flourishing and I see the Lean philosophy as the way to do that but it's going to take disciplined passion for us to uphold and continue to improvements we've made."

"It takes commitment," Tuck said.

"You're absolutely right," Nate said. "I've seen far too many businesses play around with Lean and give it up because they only made superficial changes. But, the most important commitment is the one you've made, John. Without absolute and definite leadership from the top down, an organization will never effectively make the transition."

"John, the company was doing ok. What made you decide to go to Lean?" Ron asked.

"Profit."

Hearing his name, Prophet perked up his ears, as best as a beagle puppy could.

"We were doing okay, Ron," John said. "But, we'd begun a downward spiral and with the cost cuts customers are demanding, the spiral would've gotten worse. The days of 'time and material' costing are long gone for us, and for most businesses. When I think about that inventory, I shudder. Think of what we could've done around here with a million dollars in capital to invest. Think of the waste we've all caused. That's over. We never even knew how much profit was being lost with each shipment. Now we do or will. Truly understanding our costs is the biggest benefit of Lean to me. We're not going to do any work unless we know the profit."

Hearing his name again, Prophet barked.

John broke off a crust of his pizza and gave it to Prophet. The pup sniffed of it and looked up at John.

"He wants pepperoni," Tuck said. "No crusts for him!"

"I wish our parts could bark," Ron said. "That way, we'd know if they're profitable."

Everyone laughed.

"We'll know the profit, thanks to Lean," John said, giving Prophet a piece of pepperoni. "Here's to profit!"

The End

END LETTER

Dear Readers:

ATMI is now a fully operational Lean operation and we're continually reviewing and refining the processes. It took us a solid year before the key elements were in place and working profitably for ATMI. Completely converting to Lean is a three-year process. The timeline in "Finding Prophet" has been shortened for literary purposes. However, it is true that I left the seminar early to institute Lean at ATMI and it is also true that I threw away a million dollars' worth of inventory.

The entire company operates in cells and operators are in direct contact with customers so they know about any changes, such as quality standards or quantity requirements. Our operators make go/no go calls on shipments. Our quality people are in the role of coach, not cop, and help people. It's truly a team effort. Employees also participate in a bonus compensation program tied directly to their production which includes hitting both quality and quantity standards.

ATMI has a fully utilized kan-ban system for raw materials and operators have what they need when they need it.

Being candid, it was a difficult transition and I can't stress enough how important commitment is to successful Lean implementation. Proper planning is crucial. Ours was a trial by fire and planning would've made it an easier process.

I would like to thank Aeroquip, a division of the Eaton Corporation, for their generous support and guidance in helping ATMI become Lean. Without their involvement, it would've been a much more difficult transition. They saw Lean as a means of improving their performance which extended to helping their suppliers become Lean. I am deeply indebted.

On a personal note, Norma and I are married and I've semi-retired. My son is taking over as President of ATMI and I'm confident of its continued success under his guidance. I've also earned my pilot's license and Norma and I spend a great deal of our time flying mercy medical flights.

0-595-29616-5